Wendy Beckett was born in East Gippsland but spent her formative years in Adelaide. Always interested in the theatre, she had her first play performed when she was nineteen and has since written ten more. As well as writing plays, she has worked as a school teacher, a print and radio journalist and a librettist. She has received literary grants from both the South Australian government and the Australia Council.

Wendy currently lives in Sydney and is working on a new play about the Australian artist Joy Hester. This is her first biography.

IMPRINT
lives

Peggy Glanville-Hicks

WENDY BECKETT

Angus&Robertson
An imprint of HarperCollins*Publishers*

*CollinsAngus&Robertson Publishers'
creative writing programme is
assisted by the Australia Council,
the federal government's arts
advisory and support organisation.*

AN ANGUS & ROBERTSON BOOK
An imprint of HarperCollinsPublishers

First published in Australia in 1992 by
CollinsAngus&Robertson Publishers Pty Limited (ACN 009 913 517)
A division of HarperCollinsPublishers (Australia) Pty Limited
25-31 Ryde Road, Pymble, NSW, 2073, Australia

HarperCollinsPublishers (New Zealand) Limited
31 View Road, Glenfield, Auckland 10, New Zealand

HarperCollinsPublishers Limited
77-85 Fulham Palace Road, London W6 8JB, United Kingdom

National Library of Australia
Cataloguing-in-Publication data:

Beckett, Wendy.
 Peggy Glanville-Hicks

 ISBN 0 207 17057 6.

 1. Glanville-Hicks, Peggy, 1912-1990. 2. Composers—Australia—
 Biography. 3. Women composers—Australia—Biography. I. Title.
 (Series: Imprint lives).

780.92

Cover photograph of Peggy Glanville-Hicks
hand-coloured by John Cockcroft Associates
Typeset in Australia by Midland Typesetters
Printed in Australia by Griffin Press

5 4 3 2 1
96 95 94 93 92

*For my closest friends who were never to
see this biography reach completion:
Peggy Glanville-Hicks and Peter McLean*

ACKNOWLEDGEMENTS

I would like to thank the following people for their assistance and co-operation during my research: John Cage, John Butler, Sir Yehudi Menuhin, Paul Bowles, Leonard Bernstein (d.), Jac Venza, Jac Murphy, Rolf and Caroline Backlund, Bernard and Cola Heiden, Carlos Surinach, Francis Thorn, Virgil Thomson (d.), Dr Geoffrey Bush, Sir Lennox and Lady Berkeley, Joseph Horovitz, Donald Ott, Oliver Daniels Lawrence Durrell (d.) and the Royal College of Music.

I would also like to thank Dr Beric Glanville-Hicks, Roger Glanville-Hicks, Esther Rofe, Joyce McGrath, Joel Crotty, the State Library of Victoria, the Melba Memorial Conservatorium and the Australia Council.

Special thanks are due to Barbara Mobbs, Drusilla Modjeska, Rupert Pole, Andrew Lamond, Matthew Blake, Richard Tipping, Renata Bianchi and Robert Pullan.

PREFACE

It was in 1985 that a non-Australian asked me if I knew any of the musical works of Australian composer Peggy Glanville-Hicks.

I had just arrived in London to research a play on American writer, Anaïs Nin. Lawrence Durrell, the English author with whom I had been corresponding for some years, had offered to help me in my search. In a coffee shop we had discussed at length friends and colleagues of Anaïs Nin's when he asked if I knew of Peggy Glanville-Hicks or her works? I was embarrassed to answer no. The name had lingered in the Australian musical world for years and yes I had heard it before, but no I could not call a single piece of music to mind. 'She was a friend of Anaïs in New York,' prompted Durrell. 'She was famous for *The Transposed Heads* and *Nausicaa*, and she made an opera of my play *Sappho*.'

Still I was dumbstruck. I had nothing to add. I knew little of this Australian composer. Durrell continued to fill in the blanks. She had been a much revered music critic on the *New York Herald-Tribune* for many years. She had written several important ballets and operas, and what's more she was living, like me, in Sydney. After such an embarrassing education I promised him I would look her up on my return, not only to interview her in relation to Anaïs Nin, but to acquaint myself as an Australian with the composer Americans called 'Erika Satie' or P. G.-H.

I called her up and was surprised to hear a warm inquisitive voice which halted me mid-sentence. 'You're a playwright, hmm, and what did you say your surname was, little one?' came the gilded voice down the line.

'Beckett.'

'That's exactly what I need at the moment.'

I waited perplexed.

'I'm writing a new opera with four gentlemen, you see, and I need a librettist, but not just any librettist. You'll be perfect. You must come over here at once and bring some of your plays with you.'

Summoned, I felt myself obeying. Before putting the receiver down I managed to ask: 'What is the name of the opera, Ms Glanville-Hicks?'

'*Becket*,' she laughed. 'Isn't it a riot!'

I agreed vaguely and took myself to 45 Ormond Street, Paddington, straight away.

At the front door of her little two-storey terrace I looked for a conventional doorbell, and instead found a metal meat skewer which I pulled. It set off a tinkling goat bell which was attached to the other side. Ms Glanville-Hicks came to the door, a smallish woman of middle weight. Her complexion was fair; she was wearing her hair swept up; her eyes were an intelligent sea-blue and she smiled with perfect teeth. She ushered me inside. She was wearing black trousers and a canary-yellow jumper. A gold monocle hung from a chain worn around her neck. Over the jumper she wore a tapestry-style Indian vest with a circular gold brooch and safety chain. She strode across her living room, which was of a faded opulent English appearance, and called back to me: 'Brandy, little one? I just show it the bottle, really.'

I nodded and followed behind into the kitchen which was blue and white and resembled a Greek tavern. 'Yes, thank you,' I said, trying simultaneously to make sense of the request to visit and the beautiful paintings which adorned the walls.

She produced a plate of hors d'oeuvres: prawns, corn chips, endives, sprouts; and poured soda water into the glass, topping it up with brandy. 'Just a thimbleful,' she laughed, 'to the colour topaz.'

We sat in the lounge room and she fixed me with her gaze. She spoke with the trace of a British accent, quick and articulate, embellishing explanations with wit and poetic reference. The afternoon slipped away while I was graced with stories of her career, her views on music in the twentieth century, and discussion of current political debates, literature, and the coming apocalypse in the year 2000. She laughed in a high dramatic tone which enhanced her theatrical storytelling. Peggy, as she instructed me to address her, was an aristocrat. She was not this by birth but by nature. She was an obvious talent, an intellectual and one wanted her approval. This was her hidden weapon, her charisma.

After establishing our mutual connections with Anaïs Nin and Lawrence Durrell she sat back like a prophet and said, 'I've known you a long time, haven't I?' She was referring to her belief in reincarnation. She believed that the same people journeyed through the life cycles together; that they would keep bumping into one another because their particular souls had something to learn from each other. I laughed out of uncertainty and because I thought of the tediousness of returning life after life to the company of those awful people I have never been able to get on with. Our only outward similarity was that we were both born in Victoria, completed our early schooling in Victoria, and left shortly thereafter. She was convinced there was much more. I left carrying a swag of history books and, as instructed, began work on the libretto of *Becket*. So began my weekly visits.

I would arrive at her house with the text and she would usher me to join her on the piano stool where she'd be pencilling in notes, rubbing out notes, repeating a strand of music. She might look hard into my face and say something like: 'Do you mind if I delete this word here? You must say so. Listen, do you hear what I'm doing?' She would begin to play, hunching her shoulders from side to side as she made her way down the length of the keyboard. I would listen to the music and look for the appropriate word, all the while considering the historical accuracy of the thees and thous in the text. She would use the words to find the music. Our mutual aim was to meet in the middle and compare notes at the end of each segment. In the meantime I would stare out over the baby grand piano to the stained-glass window at the side. Shafts of coloured light filtered through the room while the maestro tucked her hair up at the back and played on. She would jostle me to attention and reach over inside the piano as she played; there was a tuning wrench she adjusted as she went, improving the note midstream. She laughed at the look of surprise on my face. I laughed with her. No work is so serious that it can't be enjoyed. When the libretto was completed after four months, Peggy still had a lot of composition work ahead of her, a process she expected would take up to two years because she had problems with her sight.

In 1987 she summoned me to the house again. The call came with the same urgency as before. It was five o'clock one afternoon. No doubt she had passed the afternoon reading detective novels on the couch as she loved to do before drinks, or 'fives' as she liked to call them. She was serious and during the second glass of topaz she turned her face to me.

'I loved the plays. I would like you now to write my biography. I will tell you everything, every sordid detail,' she laughed. 'With a lady, well, one can be indiscreet.' She laughed again. 'Of course, you will read it back to me on occasion and we will make the necessary modifications, such as leaving out my middle name and any other such trivia that I deem unsuitable.'

I was dumbstruck. I had not considered this turn of events. I went home and promised to think on it for a day or two. This book is the result . . .

Slowly, over many interviews, I became the biographer of Peggy Glanville-Hicks, composer. As a playwright there is always a temptation to invent, but Peggy's life story proved to be richer than fiction. There is also a temptation to conceal. In anyone's personality there are aspects that irritate us; these are usually the same aspects that endear them to us. A biographer can ignore neither. If Mark Twain was right and we remember best those things which never actually happened to us, then this is the pattern of every artist—to recreate their own past, to colour, to exaggerate, to embellish aspects of their life. Should a biographer bestow more weight on a fact such as a marriage, or follow the subject's heart to an unknown lover? Should the biographer count over the major life events when the subject claims that the meaningful events were of the imagination? Is the biographer to attempt to get closer to the subject by uncovering their deepest thoughts or to re-record details which are readily available in the unread archives of public libraries?

It is my belief that if the subject is living, she should be invited to enjoy the process of re-entering her experiences and telling her story in whatever ways she chooses to remember them. And what greater homage is there to an artist than that they may witness their immortality in print, if only for a brief moment, *while they live*? For all stories, true or fictional, are gone as soon as they are told, if not into oblivion then into the repertoire of another storyteller, to be translated and transformed into yet another story. Stories are the inaccurate recollections of a fertile imagination. Biography too is storytelling. It is not a sterile form of journalism, rather it is a celebration of life, both real and imagined. If the subject lies to her biographer and the checking of facts fails to illuminate or dispel, then what the subject says is all there is, we have to trust her.

The linking friend between Peggy Glanville-Hicks and myself, Lawrence Durrell, put it this way: 'The artist must take the lonely path through experience in order to put life into an artistic perspective.'[1]

NOTES

1. Lawrence Durrell, in interview with the author, 1989.

THE
CONSERVATORIUM

In 1932 at the age of nineteen Peggy Glanville-Hicks bought a one-way ticket to London in the hope of securing for herself a career in music as a composer. If her aspirations were high so too were her dedication and talent, for on her arrival at the Royal College of Music she won a scholarship to study for four years with some of the most talented composers of the century.

A headstrong, naive Melbourne girl, Peggy said that she pushed herself to the front counter of the Royal College of Music, addressing the director Sir Hugh Allen who happened to be there at the time. At the first opportunity she interjected, 'I've come on a one-way ticket from Australia and I've enough money to live for about three months. What scholarships might there be?'

Sir Hugh Allen, looking a little taken aback, enquired, 'And what is your name, young lady?'

'Peggy,' she replied.

'You mean Margaret, I take it?' Sir Hugh asked.

'No, I mean Peggy,' she said.

'Oh dear,' said Sir Hugh. 'It's not a proper name. You'll never get a Christian burial!'

'I'm not interested in burials,' said Peggy, 'I'm interested in scholarships, what do you have, um, sir?'

He laughed grimly, then softened. 'Well actually we do have a scholarship, left us by a lady composer, Carlotta Rowe.'

Peggy grinned a full wide smile, handed over her musical scores and waited. Sir Hugh went into the next room to read her work, leaving Peggy on a seat at the counter. He returned within an hour, ready to make her the offer of a scholarship. But before he could speak Peggy said, 'I accept.'

This is the way Peggy told a story. She would create or recreate the dialogue and character for the telling. As a playwright I had an ear for dialogue. She teased me theatrically, never clearly distinguishing authenticity of fact. Because of this it is sometimes difficult to source the spoken quote. But together, as composer and playwright, we heard the most extraordinary stories, some real, some of Peggy's making.

Peggy Glanville-Hicks was born in Melbourne, Australia, in 1912. After the land boom of the 1880s, and with economic conditions continually improving, Melbourne had become a busy metropolis. These favourable times had brought a healthy influx of migrants and a greater and more diverse appreciation of music.

In 1911, in the year before Peggy's birth, Dame Nellie Melba had realised her ambition of heading an opera company in her own country. She and tenor John McCormack were the principal stars. In 1912, Thomas Quinlan brought from Europe what was described as the most impressive opera group ever to visit Australia. Equipped with an orchestra and a triple cast of singers, including the tenor John Coates, their first complete performance of Wagner's *Ring Cycle* was impressive. The company stayed for two seasons.[1] It was around this time that the original Melbourne Symphony Orchestra, founded in 1906 by Alberto Zelman Junior, came into its own. The establishment of a permanent symphony orchestra was the dream of every state. Melbourne was awash with music.[2]

Peggy was the only daughter of Ernest Glanville-Hicks and Myrtle King. Ernest was of Cornish descent, a practising Anglican minister who left Cornwall to preach the Bible in New Zealand. While preaching in New Zealand, Ernest met Peggy's mother Myrtle, a ceramic artist from Norfolk whose father was also a minister. The two fell in love and moved to Melbourne, where they married soon after their arrival.

From her parents Peggy learnt early the value of a career, and at the age of twelve decided to be a composer, having written several songs for herself at the family piano.

Ernest Glanville-Hicks was a reluctant minister but knew little of life outside the church. His family had thought it a suitable occupation and one that might quell his intellectual curiosity, but Ernest quickly grew tired of the Bible's 'phraseology', a word he used to describe the limitations of religious language and interpretation. He longed to address social issues more directly. He left the ministry to become a sub-editor on the Melbourne *Herald*. After a period of time as a journalist he realised all too gravely the influence of newspaper advertising and decided to return to more humanitarian pursuits. From journalism he had learned how the funds of great organisations operated and sought to turn it to the good of humankind. In 1932 at the inception of the Lord Mayor's Fund he was appointed secretary and chief executive officer. In a quarter of a century he raised over two million pounds for charity, securing for himself an OBE and the respect of Melbourne.

Despite Peggy's religious upbringing she shared none of her father's traditional Christian beliefs. Later, as a believer in reincarnation, Peggy came to abhor Western religions. 'It's a mistake,' she once said, 'there is not Father, Son and Holy Ghost. Rather there is spirit, ethereal body—as in ghosts we see and indeed the transitory guardians; and physical body, the body that is at death discarded and decays like the leaves.' An exponent of Robert Graves' *King Jesus*, Peggy subscribed to the notion that Jesus Christ did not die on the cross. Like Graves, she believed the crucifixion to have been a punitive procedure, and that the disciples of Christ whisked him away to Rome where he continued to preach as a prophet, dying at a generous old age. Peggy also studied geology and anthropology, which confirmed for her the need of a pragmatic approach to faith.

As a young girl Peggy believed there was an emotional distance between her mother and herself. She felt Myrtle preferred the company of her sons. Despite this, Peggy retained an unshakable attachment to Myrtle. This bond was to be the one thing that contradicted Peggy's belief in reincarnation. Although she sympathised with the Eastern views of religion, she was unable to relinquish the notion of her mother remaining a 'guardian angel' long after death.

Her parents encouraged her ambitions from an early age. It was always felt that Peggy was in some way gifted, and her dedication to piano lessons from the time she could first struggle up onto the piano stool were reason enough to take her seriously. Her younger brother Beric even called her 'the genius', a little peeved that he and his elder brother Garth were left to attend to domestic chores while Peggy practised.

Peggy's mother was a highly creative person who took prizes in the Melbourne show for her ceramics. She inculcated in her daughter a sense of 'purposeful ambition'. Peggy always believed that hard work was its own reward. Perhaps Peggy's mother had high ideals for her daughter; after all, she herself was a very talented woman. Peggy seemed to be discontented with an ordinary childhood, or adulthood for that matter. Perhaps the ambivalence of her familial position as the only girl generated its own pressures. It is difficult to know whether Peggy felt pushed to succeed or did so of her own volition. In any case her dedication met with special privileges and praise; this was to continue throughout her life. Peggy's relationship with her mother seems to have been one of great loyalty and respect. Peggy was proud of her Mimi, as Myrtle was known to her children, but this pride seemed to lack depth. There was a sense of distance in the family's concepts of respect and loyalty, and yet Peggy felt conditioned by them. She responded out of a measured affection. In this she identified with her mother, yet at the same time she desperately fought against the coldness she perceived to be present in her childhood. Myrtle appeared to be doting enough and yet Peggy felt she withdrew from her. It was as if Peggy could never get the attention she wanted; perhaps it was merely the outward physical affection that she felt discouraged from showing. Whatever this shortcoming was, it lingered within her, creating a nature at once warm, distant and aloof.

Peggy's elder brother Garth grew up to become an architect who, among other things, designed the Darwin Hotel (later destroyed by Cyclone Tracy). He was considered by Peggy to be both innovative and benign, that is, he didn't create the sort of things people objected to. During the Second World War he joined the AIF, like many architects, and worked in the engineering department. His main duties were to assist in the construction of bridges across waterways. The army imagined this would be of great assistance for military operations in a war zone, to speed the passage of soldiers.

While working on one bridge construction site, Garth volunteered to test some new respiratory equipment. The plan was to supervise a series of pylons being positioned twelve feet under the water. His diving helmet was a rubber concoction that served as a face mask, to which was attached a flexible hose for air intake. It is not clear which part of the apparatus failed, but after an unusually long period of time extra divers were sent down after him. Garth had drowned.

Tragedy subsequently ricocheted through his family. His wife suicided; their son had an accident which left him brain damaged and institutionalised for life; and the only remaining daughter died after developing fluid retention which was thought to have been caused, indirectly, by the contraceptive pill. Although these events could not be directly interrelated, their sequence indicates a horrific family history.

Peggy's younger brother Beric trained as a doctor and went on to become a radiologist in Melbourne. His sketch of their childhood days is quite different from Peggy's. He recalls a great deal of singing in the family home. He told me the story of their parents' courtship in the church choir in New Zealand when his father was about to take his vows. His father had recounted to him his first meeting with their mother Myrtle. The two were seated opposite each other on a train to Auckland. They had not yet been introduced. Ernest leant across from his seat and in a loud voice announced to the passengers, 'I'm going to marry her.' Myrtle, looking embarrassed, got out at the next stop.

Beric, known for his wit, described his father as 'a little man who didn't look too bad when he had his hair'. His mother he described as 'elegant, sophisticated and beautiful'. She had an outstanding voice and, according to Beric, played the piano like a concert pianist. Beric and Peggy both studied piano at a young age but a sadistic teacher dissuaded Beric from going further. He would practise the scales religiously only to be rapped across the knuckles with a large ebony ruler for every minor hesitation. Fearful of further recriminations he took up football instead. Beric said: 'Piano, well it was Peggy who was going to be a genius, or so Mimi said.'

He described his sister as an ordinary child whose only exceptional quality, other than the piano, was her ability to get out of doing her share of the housework.

> Brother Garth and I always got stuck with the washing up while precious Peg would thump away at the piano hour after hour. Mimi would even prepare water bottles filled with warm water to soothe her hands during practice. There was nothing Mimi wouldn't do for Peggy. However, she was not the cuddling type and so perhaps Peggy felt Mimi didn't show her love for her. I knew Peggy felt this way but her career was Mimi's life. Peggy was home so rarely, what with boarding school and then her overseas education, but Mimi was aware of her every movement and encouraged her as much as she could.[3]

Many of the Glanville-Hicks family share a common birthday, the twenty-ninth of December. They include Myrtle, Peggy, her brother Beric, her aunt, and, later, her great-niece. This oddity has been often celebrated by the Melbourne newspapers.

From Barclay Street, St Kilda, where Peggy was born, the family moved to Elwood, where she attended kindergarten. There she befriended her first playmate, Tim. Peggy believed he was already a painter at six, but his life was cut short when he climbed upon a tar truck that was mending a nearby road. He slipped and fell into the tar. Peggy, when she heard, was so shocked she fainted and had to be kept in bed for several days. She remembered this incident as an omen, an experience of loss, too early for understanding. She would often retell the experience. In later years when she met the charming composer and author Paul Bowles, she claimed he looked exactly the same as Tim. Oddly enough this lifetime friend was to be another type of twin: born on the thirtieth of December, by Australian time and Peggy's reckoning, he shared her famous family birthday.

The family moved several times after Elwood following the needs of Ernest's work, finally settling at 442 Barkers Road, Hawthorn, where Myrtle had purchased a block of land. Myrtle set about designing a Georgian mansion with the help of Melbourne architects Stevenson and Meldron. The house consisted of a single storey and although highly functional, in keeping with Myrtle's temperament, it stood amongst scarlet-flowering eucalypts. Peggy lived here from the age of twelve and attended the Methodist Ladies College at the bottom of the hill. Her parents later sent her, as a full time boarder, to Clyde—a much respected school at Mount Macedon, Victoria, later made famous by the film *Picnic at Hanging Rock*. Peggy described Clyde to me.

After Melbourne Mount Macedon was wide and flat and plain. My first impression was that I might not enjoy it at all. But in no time I became aware of the mystic lake, the clouds that drifted in so low, jutting out above the famous hanging rock, it was heaven! Sometimes we girls would be taken on camping trips there. We would wake in the morning with snow on our pillows. I can't say I was brilliant but I came top in everything except mathematics and sport. In sport I was very careful to make a deliberate fool of myself so that I *wouldn't* be chosen for the hockey team. Out there pushing that silly ball around was not what I wanted to do!

The militancy, dressing in black dinner jackets and skirt for the evening meal, then prayers. The headmistress, Miss Tucker, was a most formidable creature. She eventually went round the bend and had to be locked up.

It was at Clyde, under the care of music teacher Mrs Noall, that Peggy first learnt about repertoire. Mrs Noall, known ungraciously to her students as Mrs Know-All, had a little wooden cottage at the back of the school where the students would be sent to practise. Initially Peggy was permitted to practise piano for a set period of twenty minutes but was later granted additional time thanks to Mrs Noall's enthusiasm. Later Peggy said, 'I wanted to be a composer not a pianist. They never understood this or refused to listen; even Mrs Noall seemed fazed.'

Composition was not considered a likely profession for a young lady in the 1920s, it was viewed as rather a girlish fancy. This, coupled with the strictness of Clyde, left little hope for Peggy's ambitious career in music.

'In childhood I was just practising for life,' Peggy said. 'I wasn't lonely really, I was just alone. Even later in marriage I was alone. I am by nature a loner, or if it was an influence I can't remember when it was that it happened to me.' But Peggy did make one friend at Clyde, Joan Watt, whom she described as: 'beautiful, with hair like silk and the longest lashes. She was so small and clever.' Joan went along with Peggy's plans to get a detention in order to avoid the dreaded sporting activities, one of which included scampering down the hanging rock itself. 'It looked like a rock sticking up out of the sea and both Joan and I imagined that we would fall clear off.'

In the twenties all young girls given to common colds or minor chest infections were thought to be in danger of contracting tuberculosis, and both Peggy and Joan fell into this category. Treatment at the time included placing the child outside at night to sleep in the open air. Joan and Peggy enjoyed this because it meant that camping trips were recommended for those thought to be inclined towards tuberculosis. Peggy joked, 'Joan, like me, had a tendency to lung trouble or so they said. How one could have a tendency one can only imagine—but for this imposition we were often subjected to an oversupply of fresh air.'

Clyde was regarded as a finishing school, but Peggy's frustration and musical aspirations got the better of her and the school failed to create a lady out of the precocious girl. She once threw a duster at a teacher whom she claimed threw it first. The teacher screamed and ran out of the room. Peggy was severely reprimanded. One of the great mysteries for Peggy and Joan was the 'Haunted Tower' which architecturally made up the main building of the school. Peggy the pragmatist explained to Joan that she 'had never actually seen or heard the ghost' which was supposed to live there. This game of make-believe caused endless shrieks of delight. It also cost them another detention.

Peggy was single-minded about music and never doubted her destiny. She wrote a piece of music around this time which she described as being a 'completely unconscious act'. As if driven by some inner compulsion to write music, and imbued with a belief in herself as a composer, Peggy felt a sense of predestination. Stifled by Clyde and longing for a fuller education in music she told her mother that all she needed to know about were treble clefs! Myrtle decided to bring her home to Hawthorn. There she returned to her practice, much to the annoyance of everyone in the house. Her brothers, according to Beric, believed her to be quite obsessed. Peggy played for hours on end, often repeating scales as if competing with an invisible demon. Recognising her daughter's commitment, Myrtle arranged for Peggy to study at the Albert Street Conservatorium. Peggy was overjoyed. Her first teacher was to be Fritz Hart, who was already a well known composer, having written twenty-two operas and several hundred songs.

Established in 1895, the Albert Street Conservatorium had had two previous names: the University Conservatorium of Music, known to students as the Melbourne Con; and the

Marshall-Hall Conservatorium. Situated in the old Victorian Artists' Association building in Albert Street, East Melbourne, it remained known as the Albert Street Con to all its students until some time after the arrival of Fritz Hart's new staff member, Dame Nellie Melba. It was the first conservatorium established in Australia, and its foundation was regarded as a major event in Australian musical history. Fritz Hart was well respected and his enthusiasm, literary ability, academic and musical achievements, and high ideals made him the obvious candidate to succeed Marshall-Hall, the founder, as director. He filled the position from 1913 to 1936.[4] Peggy would later say of Fritz Hart: 'He was neglected because he was Australian, because he was around, and therefore under-valued like a plentiful commodity. Australia always looked to Italy and Germany in pursuit of excellence in opera.'

Albert Street Con was known for its purity of musical ideal, of which Fritz Hart was a great exemplar. It was no surprise, then, that Dame Nellie Melba felt an immediate affection for the institution and, under the directorship of Hart, the Melba school of singing began to take up a large part of the Con's program, with the desired repercussion of expanding both the school's curriculum and student enrolments.

Peggy was fortunate enough to enter the Albert Street Conservatorium in its thirty-sixth year, 1930, and enjoy the energy of these exciting times. Her educational program consisted of singing under the direction of Dame Melba, along with pianoforte, cello, violin, viola, clarinet and oboe lessons. In addition, Fritz Hart himself instructed her in harmony, counterpoint, elements of music, ear training, prosody (the setting of words), and composition. Other composition classes included form and analysis, history and aesthetics, interpret-ation of works, ensemble class, operatic class, choral class and English. Elocution and special dramatic classes were also conducted along with physical training and personal hygiene, deportment, callisthenics, dancing, Italian and French.[5] Interestingly enough the honorary secretary to the council of the Melbourne Conservatorium of Music, as the Albert Street

Conservatorium was then known, was none other than Ernest Glanville-Hicks, Peggy's father. She never once mentioned his interest in music nor did she ever explain his position on the council. Perhaps she never knew?

Peggy later destroyed a large number of her early musical scores from this period, embarrassed by their naivety. One such piece, 'A Prelude to an Infant Protégé' mysteriously found its way into an American publisher's hands when Peggy was in her thirties. She was extremely amused and the piece happily vanished again.

In 1980 Peggy offered some insights into this period:

We were always pressed into being pianists because that seemed tangible . . . From an early age it was songs and opera that interested me as a composer; especially prosody. The singer needs the composer to be adept in prosody. Fritz (Hart) would have me walk around the room reciting the words aloud, a habit I practised continuously throughout my composing career . . . A high emphatic note is something that can be swallowed in the sentence; that way you can pass on to the real words in a sentence. One needs to be a writer, a poet, a composer to know how and when the words rise and fall . . . like speech, except widened. English is difficult to set. A syllable per note, German is easier. Italian is easiest to set and sing . . . The words only need a mood or an idea you like. The rhythm in the text will determine the melody. Melodic sentence almost dictates . . . but not always. Every aspect is malleable until frozen . . . It's a gift, prosodic art. A feeling for literature is necessary.

The training she received was to be of great advantage later in her career as a composer. The high standards set by the Conservatorium provided her with a solid basis technically, a quality she was later praised for by both critics and composers.[6]

After completing her studies at the Conservatorium, Peggy set her sights on the Royal College of Music. Fritz Hart had been a graduate of the Royal College, and every music student dreamed of studying under such musical giants as Malcolm Sargent and Ralph Vaughan Williams. Australia must have seemed undeveloped musically compared to England, America and Europe. The *Australian Musical News*, a popular publication with music lovers Australia-wide, was filled with stories and pictures of the big time overseas.

In 1931 Peggy took up the challenge and set off on a one-way ticket to London in the hope of uncovering that wealth. In support of her decision and to celebrate the successful completion of her studies at the Albert Street Conservatorium, a farewell concert was held in her honour. A poster was pasted up across Melbourne showing the shining young face of the budding composer. Peggy objected to the poster's wording, which billed her as a 'young composer-pianiste'. 'The "e" on the end of the pianist is the problem,' she said. But it was too late to change it and a crowd of some five hundred people gathered on the night of the concert. Reviews appeared in the entertainment pages of the Melbourne daily newspapers. It proved to be a huge success, with Miss Gertrude Healy playing a violin composition of Peggy's and a Miss Beatrice Oakley singing three of Peggy's songs. In addition to playing the piano solo in the first movement of Mozart's Concerto in D Minor, Peggy, backed by the Melbourne Symphony Orchestra, played three preludes for piano of her own composition

This was the beginning of the career that Peggy had longed for. Packed and heading up the gangplank of the ship *Mongolia* on 13 June 1931, she was heard to call out to her friends and family waving at the dock: 'Don't hold your breath!'

NOTES

1. Bernard Grun, *The Timetables of History*, Simon & Schuster, New York, 1982.
2. Isabelle Moresby, *Australia Makes Music*, Longmans Green and Co., London, 1948, pp. 5–7.

3. Dr Beric Glanville-Hicks in interview with the author, Melbourne, 1988.
4. *Melba Memorial Conservatorium of Music 30th Year*, National Press Printers, Melbourne, 1930; *Australian Musical News*, 1 February 1933.
5. Ibid.
6. James Melon Interview, State Library of Victoria, 18 February 1980.

ROYAL
COLLEGE OF MUSIC

The true story behind Peggy Glanville-Hicks' scholarship to the Royal College of Music differs from her version. Before leaving the Albert Street Conservatorium in Melbourne, Peggy was runner-up for the Clarke Scholarship in Victoria. Jas Dyer, a woman who was acting mayor in Melbourne at the time, forwarded to London a set of ten of Peggy's compositions, including choral, pianoforte, violin and orchestral work. These were sent to Sir Hugh Allen, in the hope that a scholarship could be awarded for Peggy to study there.[1] Peggy would no doubt have known of this arrangement but did not at any time acknowledge Jas Dyer's assistance.

Royal College scholarships were competitive and Peggy had to compete with talent drawn from throughout the United Kingdom. It is not known whether she was awarded the scholarship after everyone else had already entered, and succeeded due to exceptional musical talent; whether the story of Sir Hugh has some truth or is a complete fabrication. Whatever the circumstances one can be sure that musical expertise would have been a primary factor in her acceptance, especially as there were few women in the field at the time. The Carlotta Rowe Scholarship for women, which Peggy did indeed win, was new at the Royal College that year, 1931. It had an annual value of £85.[2] Speculating on comments made later about her, her success was almost certainly due to her skill in composition and pianoforte work, which would have placed her ahead of other competitors.

At the Royal College of Music she studied under Ralph Vaughan Williams and R. O. Morris. Her piano studies were conducted by Arthur Benjamin, an Australian whose opera *The Devil Take Her* had been a tremendous success in London

14

the previous year. Benjamin also taught her orchestration. Other teachers for conducting and piano were Constant Lambert and Sir Malcolm Sargent.

The Royal College of Music has always been a prestigious institution. Founded by the Prince of Wales (later Edward VII) and incorporated by Royal Charter in 1883, the president of the college is always a member of the royal family. Since 1952 this position has been held by Her Majesty Queen Elizabeth, the Queen Mother. From the outside the building has an imposing Victorian presence not unlike a cathedral. Facilities during Peggy's internship included a spacious concert hall, built in 1903 for major concerts and performances. There was also residential accommodation available for students, although this remained the prerogative of wealthy country pupils. Peggy opted for local accommodation as did most of her colleagues; usually this consisted of share flats or a bed-sitting room.[3]

Lessons were conducted on a one-to-one basis, with the exception of musicianship and history classes, which were taught in small tutorials. Tuition was available in a wide range of subjects depending on staff expertise at the time. A significant number of guest lecturers brought welcome change to the syllabus throughout the year. Ensemble activities were encouraged and Peggy developed a particular interest in chamber choir music though the composer's group was her most valued class.

Every term recitals, prize competitions and lectures would be open to attendance and there was a high level of interest in these. There were also visits from eminent musicians. It was possible to receive special, remedial or additional coaching in almost any area the student was deficient in. The college encouraged the pursuit of excellence, that is, a high pass mark in all areas, and if one was fortunate enough to be accepted, the path ahead was potentially attractive and successful. The student was immersed in music. If saturation set in early there was every chance the latent, well-rounded musician, composer or conductor would emerge.

Peggy was insatiable and savoured every minute, especially the chance to learn from guest lecturers, with whom she tended to be overly impressed. Within course work a student was expected to attend all lessons. Should a student not comply with college requirements then tenure could be terminated. Peggy regarded each lesson by a lecturer or composer as an intellectual opportunity and her record of attendance was impeccable.

Peggy's ship arrived in London on 21 July 1931. She found her new environment very exciting after Melbourne. She found accommodation in a studio apartment just off Cheyne Walk in Cheslea, and was delighted to find she was living opposite the author A. A. Milne with whom her father had been acquainted. Peggy and A. A. Milne lunched together on occasion at Ye Old Cheshire Cheese, a local pub. Constant Lambert, who also lived nearby, invited her to a promenade concert at which he was conducting his *Rio Grande*. Other concerts she attended in her first few weeks included *The Planets* conducted by Gustav Holst, whom she met after the concert with composers Rutland Boughton and Ralph Vaughan Williams.

Everyone was encouraging and in no time at all her knowledgeable conversation and small compositions began to attract attention. One supporting comment of the time came from the composer Cyril Scott who said of her, 'She has something very definite to say through her compositions and her piano'. As a former student of Fritz Hart in Melbourne, her level of expertise, especially in the handling of prosody, was her special gift. A cabled message to Melbourne newspapers in the winter of 1931 told of these exciting developments and of her associations with the famous. Her scholarship success was the best news of all. It was to be renewed annually for five years subject to satisfactory achievement.[4]

During her first year of study at the Royal College of Music, Peggy made friends with composers Esther Rofe, Benjamin Britten and Stanley Bate. Esther Rofe, an Australian composer and former student of Fritz Hart's, became Peggy's best friend and often studied with her. In an interview at her Melbourne home in 1988 Esther recalled the college years of their friendship with great fondness. She described their first meeting. 'When I first saw her I heard myself say aloud: "She is almost beautiful". She had Bambi eyes, grey eyes like Seymour Hicks. An impish face, a slightly turned up nose, oh and yes plenty of boyfriends. Such a personality. And to top it off she came from my home town, Melbourne. I just knew we were going to hit it off.'

Esther marvelled at Peggy's capabilities.

> She was such a clever girl, she always got what she wanted and met whom she wanted. Confident and competent always, she had an excellent sense of timing both in her music life, her personal life and indeed her career. Peggy cued herself to events and always had something ready for the right festival or production. If there was a Greek festival, sure enough she would have a piece of Greek-fashioned music at the ready. She was a professional.

Esther hesitated for a moment, her timidity apparent, then continued,

> Peggy was never afraid to speak her mind, even to the critics. She demanded that they [the critics] attend performances early in a production season or not at all. She recognised the importance of reviews and their impact if published early. She knew that mere newspaper coverage was insufficient and that reviews published on the second last night of production, as was often the case, were commercially useless. This incensed her and she let her rage be felt. She could do that, you know, talk up a storm and get everyone's attention.

During the interview Esther remembered her friend's personality with fondness. Her face conveyed an air of satisfaction. I could sense she wanted to say something useful and accurate about Peggy's music. I hadn't posed the question but the composer was sifting through her memory, hoping to be honest rather than impressive. 'Peggy's songs were rather beautiful. They had a mystic quality, an *other* quality. They were removed. They were a mood that came and passed by. They had impact always because they were of her.'

During the first month of college Peggy was assigned to work with Esther. She would arrive at Esther's house laden down with scores and a wry expression on her face that pleaded 'help me'. Esther would lead her in by the hand and the two would set to work, studying, copying parts and arranging orchestration. Esther, who was more experienced in orchestration and part-writing, found herself annoyed by Peggy's attitude. Peggy, having appealed to Esther's goodwill for assistance, had the nerve to feign restlessness, and was eager and fidgety to finish. 'She wanted to intellectualise perfectly acceptable musical facts,' Esther said.

Peggy had difficulty in coping with Esther's insistence that music time-changes from two-four to six, eight to five, four to seven, fourths, and so on, could occur. Esther took great pains to explain that one could not get a large number of bars into orchestral work and yet, she still had to check and double check Peggy's work. Esther feared Peggy's rebelliousness might get the better of her. 'She would only put the effort in according to her own assessment.' For example, Peggy would placidly say 'Ah, put in 173 bars,' causing great shrieks of despair from Esther, followed by riotous laughter once she had caught on to the tease. Peggy considered these study assignments boring. Esther recognised in Peggy a mercurial temperament. Despite being a perfectionist in her compositions she could also be indifferent. She destroyed much of her early work because she thought it inferior. Esther would scold her like a mother hen. Esther was twenty-seven at the time, Peggy just nineteen.

They shared a common interest in painting and art exhibitions and frequented the numerous salons and galleries of London. Peggy herself dabbled with painting and Esther was encouraging, although she described Peggy as being 'susceptible to colour' as if it were an illness. They had long debates about whether shadows were grey, as Esther perceived them, or navy blue as Peggy described them. Peggy was more definite and out of boredom Esther would defer to Peggy's ego. Nevertheless, the two were often observed by friends bickering, debating and laughing, arm in arm.

After music, politics and world affairs were their favourite topics of discussion. Peggy had peculiar socialist views about benevolently changing the lot of underdeveloped countries, and Esther loved to temper her opinion by creating obstacles and offering contrary points of view. Esther would lean forward on her chair, clutching at Peggy's arm, trying to impress upon her the difficulty of political change. 'You'd have anarchy,' she'd warn, a bewildered expression growing on her face.

Peggy always preferred to sit outside where possible, even at friends' houses. This was partly because of her smoking habit. She smoked a dainty little silver pipe, and drank Scotch whisky while Esther 'kept her company' with a hot cup of tea. At parties, Esther would niggle at Peggy for spoiling her fruit cup. Peggy would slip in the spirits while she wasn't looking and then when Esther awoke in the morning with a blinding headache, chastise her for being a drinker. Before one such party, Esther asked Peggy to help with preparations. Peggy hastily swept the cigarette butts under the carpet and tossed magazines behind pillows. During the party, while everyone was dancing, Esther stumbled over a bump of cigarette butts in the carpet and sprawled full face across the dining room floor. Unwillingly, Esther became a partner to Peggy's antics and humour. Their odd friendship survived many separations over the years. 'Ah, Peggy Glanville-Hicks,' said Esther, 'I've heard that name all my life!'

Esther witnessed the arrival on the scene of the dashing English composer Stanley Bate, whom Peggy later married. 'Stanley,'

Esther said, 'was described by almost everyone who knew him as beautiful at a time when the most a gentleman could hope to be called was handsome.'

Peggy regarded Bate as a genius, as did many of his contemporaries. He was capable of writing several symphonies in just a few weeks and though much of what he composed wasn't usable, there was a general consensus that he had the skill and speed to become one of England's great composers. Many compared him to the young Benjamin Britten.

Esther regarded him and his work as facile and was irritated by Peggy's sycophantic tendencies with him and her praise of him. She was was enraged to discover that Peggy spent some of her precious time during college semester copying parts for him. The resulting argument between Peggy and Esther almost caused a falling out. Esther inferred that Peggy was selling herself short by helping Bate. Esther knew of Peggy's admiration for Stanley but felt a need to protect her. She distrusted Stanley and suspected he had hidden motives. 'Peggy,' Esther said, 'had a belief at this age that men needed help and she was obsessed by Bate.' Their argument over Bate never really ended, surfacing between the women as late as 1990. Esther could never accept Peggy's deferral to Bate as more talented, worthy or deserving.

The two women often disagreed. In 1990 Esther travelled from Melbourne to Sydney to stay with Peggy for a week. One of their typical discussions took place. They shouted each other down with opposing views about a theatrical production that they had both been engaged in thirty years before. Esther made a throwaway line about Bate's inferiority to Peggy, and Peggy almost conceded that she was the more lasting historically. This was an odd modesty for Peggy, whose healthy ego had been noticed from a young age. She offered her defence, 'But you have to agree that Stanley was beautiful'. The two women then made a 'baa' sound like bleating goats and continued with the thread of the story which had originally focused on the theatre.

While both women were still students, they went on

weekend trips away. Peggy remembered one trip to Dorking in the English countryside where they visited their teacher Ralph Vaughan Williams. Peggy was dressed in a brown tailored suit with black velvet lapels and cuffs. Esther wore a light floral dress with tassels at the neck and a quaint bow on the back pleat. In a photograph of this outing Esther seems very pleased with her appearance. Both women wore autumn hats with black bands and a sensible pair of gloves. Esther had an attack of nerves on the journey and Peggy tried to demystify Vaughan Williams, explaining that he dressed like a gentleman farmer on weekends; but Esther could not be pacified. Vaughan Williams was waiting by the gate for them. He was dressed as Peggy had said, in gardening trousers and old carpet slippers. Esther stared at his shoes. He ushered them inside. His comfortable country house was filled with cats and books, which delighted Esther. He invited them to a game of 'miss and giggle' at which Esther looked predictably anxious. He was referring to a game of tennis.

After an exhausting day and dinner, where Peggy excelled, the two women retired to their room at the back of the house. They sat propped up in their single beds both wearing flannelette nighties, discussing some of the ideas shared earlier with Vaughan Williams. Peggy puffed away on her silver pipe and Esther became indignant. Irritated by the smoke, she tried in vain to appeal to Peggy's good manners about smoking in bed. After a minor altercation Peggy took up her pipe again and turned the conversation to music. As always, Peggy got her way.

Esther was an uneasy visitor and a nervous social mixer, but Peggy drew her out bit by bit. Peggy knew only too well the value of professional associations, and courted a great many influential composers. Her desire to be among the wild and talented was not only an opportunist tendency; she had come a long way to join the world of musicians. She had a need to be accepted and taken seriously, even in her first year of college. She had a sense of having just this one chance of success and she was determined not to lose it. She told

Esther of her aspirations to be as great a composer as Vaughan Williams. At times Esther was shocked by her ambition.

Peggy found it easy to make new acquaintances. She was friendly and welcoming. She was fascinated above all by talent and there seemed to be no shortage in London. Benjamin Britten was one such talent. Britten was not a student at the college but was a familiar face in the student musical set. Peggy and he became friends and spent many hours chatting over the opera, the ballet and theories of prosody. Peggy already had her sights set on writing an opera, perhaps the most challenging task for any composer, and especially a student composer. Britten was fascinated by the bold Australian. Peggy believed he found an arrogance in her that was challenging or shocking. She couldn't be sure which. She delighted in teasing him. She would dismiss his musical heroes just to elicit a response.

Peggy enjoyed the drama of associating with famous people. It was part of her teasing nature to re-enact experiences shared with them. She was even known to select a particular piece of music on occasion before telling a favourite story. She especially liked to play both roles, keeping the dialogue of herself and her subject as authentic as possible. One such story was about Benjamin Britten. It began with him working on an opera. They had been discussing its structure for two hours and Peggy had become irritated.

'You've no training in prosody,' she said, as if she had a monopoly on the art.

'But Peggy,' replied Britten, 'I have other gifts. In time, in time.'

'You're absolutely hopeless,' she restated. Britten was oddly charmed by her disrespect, and she laughed at the retelling.

Britten introduced Peggy to Stravinsky. Peggy already thought of herself as taking a neo-classicist path. She was influenced by Stravinsky, Hindemith and Bartók; less so by Schoenberg, whom she regarded as the last of the romantics. She felt Schoenberg's roots were too deeply embedded in atonalism. Stravinsky, Britten and Peggy met in a bar on one of her European trips. She returned to Britain a little disgruntled and told Esther that she thought Stravinsky 'A little man with quick nervous movements, a surprising person who disliked talking about music!' She complained that he had only wanted to talk of French poetry and not the beloved music that she had so expected to hear about. She became enraged in the retelling of the story and condemned him to Esther. Britten, also present, was amused by her naivety and purist attitudes, while at the same time appreciating her need for serious discussion. Peggy threw a dishcloth at him and Esther became quite hysterical at her rudeness. Britten seemed to find satisfaction and joy in the conversations he shared with Peggy, and for a time he played the role of big brother. Esther was suspicious of Britten's intentions, as she had been of Stanley Bate's. There was to be a gap of some years before Peggy and Britten met again. Britten's career frequently took him abroad, while Peggy's studies began to claim an even greater portion of her time.

The 1920s were characterised musically by what was known to its adepts as 'contemporary music'. This comprised the twelve-tone school, seated in Vienna with an outpost in Berlin, and the neo-classicists or School of Paris. By the 1930s neo-romanticism became popular also. Each of these phases were contemporaneous with painting movements of the same name. Looking back, Peggy saw herself as belonging to the thirties and forties yet, in keeping with tradition, was required to study from the earlier schools of music. Schoenberg had had a profound influence on the musical students of Peggy's generation but the music of the late thirties and forties returned increasingly to a melodic structure. Peggy borrowed some elements from each period, avoiding some of the more melodic structures. Twentieth century composers were, according to Peggy, backward-looking. A likeminded music critic, Virgil Thomson, explained this retrospective tendency in more depth, saying, 'Paul Hindemith evoked the baroque, Stravinsky and Schoenberg were both working within the traditional octave and Bartók sought the inclusion of the folk elements. All of these men seemed to find their roots in music of a former time.'[5] Peggy did not see herself as backward-looking and yet she called herself neo-classicist in her formative years.

Schoenberg's influences were evident in some of Peggy's later music. She based much of her work in traditional octave structures but often added a percussion element. The use of rhythm, texture and phrasing could be deemed classical. Were it not for her foray into harsher expressionist idioms of an Eastern flavour the work could be described as conventional. While still a student, she believed that by removing harmony as a modulating part of formal structure, new needs became apparent and these necessitated additional structural change. This became an area of enormous intrigue for her. She, like her contemporaries, moved through the musical influence of the thirties and forties, but unlike those who returned to melody via the Schoenberg influence, Peggy hoped to incorporate other elements. She thought she might even go the way of Bartók. Benjamin Britten was her ally in this, believing himself to be a neo-classicist at the time. Esther listened to their endless conversations and looked on like a loving sister but did not identify herself with any of their definitions.

By the end of the first year of her study Peggy was beginning to realise some of her musical ideals. She was also developing an awareness of politics and the world she lived in. This was a time of change for her, of growing up. She saw the importance of changing direction and of finding her own musical style and persona. When Esther returned to Australia because her mother was ill and Britten left on tour, Peggy found herself unexpectedly lonely and without the comfort of a female companion or close friend.

During the summer vacation, when most of the college's music students returned home, Peggy remained in Britain. It was too far and too expensive to go home to Australia. She decided to take a course at Oxford. Throughout her Royal College education she took several courses there during vacations. It was during this summer vacation, while studying archaeology and international politics, that she befriended a young Indian woman.

'She was one of the plainest, ugliest women I had ever seen,' said Peggy, 'but in her eyes there was an unquenchable flame.' This was to be her last negative comment about her new friend Indira Gandhi. With Esther in Australia, Indira became Peggy's confidante and friend, often inviting her home to dine with the family. Indira was studying international politics and although Peggy only shared some components of this subject area, music and politics were often discussed at the same table. Indira was already part of India's passive resistance movement. Her father, Jawaharlal Nehru, led a great many movements in opposition to British rule. Indira's involvement in the struggle often meant that she spent more time in prison and in court than she did studying. Peggy would keep copies of the lecture notes for her or collect them from other students. Peggy remembered how Indira changed after imprisonment or political defeat, becoming more militant intellectually and somehow hardened.

In 1933 Peggy visited India with Indira. The year before, Gandhi had been arrested and the Indian Congress declared illegal. Freed, he suspended the civil disobedience campaign in India. The All-India Congress Party was to wait three or four more years before winning elections.

The year 1933 was one of crisis and change, not only in India. Adolf Hitler was appointed Germany's Chancellor, with Goebbels as his minister for propaganda, and the first concentration camps were erected in Germany. The boycott of the Jews had begun. Three years later ten million prisoners had been interned there. Also in 1933 the USA drew up the Twenty-first Amendment repealing Prohibition.

There was much to talk about the night the two women attended Government House in India, but for all the history in the making initially it seemed that some unstated agreement had ordained that the evening be a domestic one with easy and friendly conversation.

'The conversations were tame really for resisters!' said

Peggy. 'Nehru, with his handsome good manners, leant across the table towards me and caught me mid-sentence as I was discussing my admiration for Greece, a country I knew little of and said, "I hear the last election in Greece was fixed."' Peggy sat there staring. 'I don't think it. I know it,' he continued.

Peggy was momentarily distracted by the Indian music in the background. She was thinking about the raga, the melodic base in Indian classical music. Despite her silence both Mahatma Gandhi and Nehru waited for her response. They expected an opinion. They went on to discuss the role of England in the new India. Peggy felt increasingly inadequate. The debate grew and the two men reasoned over English principles of 'divide and rule'. Peggy made vague gestures of agreement, unsure of how she was being received, thinking that in this household she was a misfit, a young Australian woman who spoke of strange issues like Australian independence. Indira was sitting at the opposite end of the table and could be heard above the others by this time. Peggy deferred to the louder conversation: 'We must attempt to heal this wound between Moslems and Hindus or it will be our greatest tragedy. We cannot shoot our way to freedom,' Indira shouted. The conversation fell silent and Nehru rose from the table and left, seemingly offended by the tone the evening was taking.

On the way home Indira explained to Peggy the importance of India developing English as its common language. Indira believed that the regional languages could be retained, but saw the desirability of a common language, uniting the states, one to the other and to the whole of the outside world.

Peggy felt that Indira knew well the danger of her political convictions. Her imprisonments coupled with her outspokenness indicated a difficult future. Peggy said, 'Indira in her twenties spoke almost prophetically of her future, awake with the knowledge that one day her beliefs would cost her her life.'

Towards the end of the second year of Peggy's study Indira

returned to India permanently and Peggy busied herself with her studies at the Royal College of Music. Her mother promised to visit from Australia. Peggy was to turn twenty-one in the December of 1933.

Leopold Stokowski, who is best known for his arrangements for Walt Disney's *Fantasia*, was a guest lecturer at the Royal College of Music during Peggy's second year. One of the first conductors to take a technical interest in recorded and broadcast music, he was experimenting with stereo recordings. During one of his advanced conducting classes, the musicians were positioning themselves in anticipation of the great conductor's lead. When the usual drummer failed to appear, Peggy was secretly moved into his chair. Twenty minutes into the piece Stokowski called the music to a standstill.

'Who's on drums?' he bellowed.

There was a deathly silence. Peggy rose shakily from the pits: 'It's me sir.'

'Stay right where you are. You're a fraction ahead of the piece. Anticipation of the rhythm is perfect. Play on.'

After this incident Peggy was in demand even more than she had imagined, and played drums on a number of occasions. As a composer she had a great love of percussion instruments, and incorporated them into her scores.

The music written by Peggy during her college years from 1931 to 1936 was substantial for a junior composer. It included an operatic work in 1934 titled *Caedmon* for which she also wrote the libretto. It was an opera in three acts for soloist, chorus and orchestra, of forty minutes duration. During 1934 she also wrote a ballet entitled *Hylas and the Nymphs*. Designed for flute, harp, strings and percussion, it had a brief playing time of fifteen minutes. Her orchestral work, although limited, included a fourteen-minute piece for orchestra titled Sinfonietta No. 1, which was also produced in 1934.

Her choral works date back to 1931, her first year at the

college, and include: *Choral Suite*, a work published by Lyrebird Press, which has been used many times over, in theatre and film; *Pastoral*; *Aria Concertante*; *Poem for Chorus and Orchestra*; and *Songs for Summer*.

Her chamber works for the 1931–1935 period were *Preludes for Piano*, *Violin Fantasy* and *First Trio for Pandeen*. Her rigorous study program took up five days a week, and weekends often found her practising and experimenting with new arrangements. She also took in copying work for established composers including Ralph Vaughan Williams, her teacher, who found a willing and capable copyist in the enthusiastic Peggy.[6]

Lessons with Ralph Vaughan Williams were Peggy's favourite and she relished every detail of the composer's conversation. This was even before she and Esther had been invited to his house. She recalled how he once glanced over a piece of her work and commented, 'I'm not mad about the piece but,' he hesitated, 'the prosody, ah! Your old teacher in Australia has trained you well.' He was referring to Fritz Hart from the Albert Street Conservatorium in Melbourne.

This praise launched Peggy into explaining the process she had learnt from Fritz Hart of walking around the room singing each word aloud. She demonstrated. Vaughan Williams was bewildered. She began to sing loudly. Vaughan Williams' attention was focused on her, so she stopped and explained: 'The word needs only a mood or an idea you like. Like Gilbert and Sullivan, rat catchers' music, masters of prosody. If the voice is going up and the excitement is going up, the idea is building to a climax; the orchestra goes up too and to hell with pianissimo, let the singers come through! Accompaniment has its importance but each part should be heard equally.'[7]

Vaughan Williams offered a smile of encouragement but didn't speak. Peggy recomposed herself, a little unsure as to whether she had gone too far. Vaughan Williams chortled and left for his next class.

Ralph Vaughan Williams wore the status of English

composer with ease; he was a creator of symphonies, operas, and songs. Himself a former student of the college, he was the perfect role model to his students and was seen as something of a celebrity by them. He had ideas of freeing English music from the more Germanic traditions to forge a fresh modal style of music. Tall, broad-shouldered, with a moderate rural English accent, he wore tailored English tweeds. Regarded as father and mentor by many of his pupils, he was known affectionately behind his back as Uncle Ralph (pronounced Rafe). According to Peggy, he often said to his pupils, 'I'm here to wait and watch. I don't teach composition. I help you to get there.'

One of Vaughan Williams' favourite examples of perfect grammar was: 'This is something up with which I will not put.' He liked to use it because it sounded incorrect. Teacher John Ireland was standing by when Peggy first received this line in reprimand and he interjected, 'Your grammar, Ralph, is absolutely correct,' winking in Peggy's direction. Peggy grinned. Vaughan Williams stood back; his judgement was in jeopardy. Pipe in hand he spoke quietly, 'I've had a lot of students, dozens of them, but very few from whom I expect a distinguished result.' As was his habit he immediately left the room, pleased at having had the last word. Esther Rofe was bowled over by this incident, never having been lucky enough to raise a glimpse of praise from the formidable composer herself. It was college gossip for months.

Already a major composer, Vaughan Williams somehow found time to continue working while teaching. During the years 1931 to 1934 the sixty-three-year-old composer was hard at work on several pieces, including Symphony No. 4 in F major, his Piano Concerto in C major, and *In Windsor Forest*, a cantata. He also produced *Fantasia on Greensleeves* for orchestra during this phase, and numerous other works.

Peggy was employed by Vaughan Williams as a copyist for a three month stint. She lived and worked at Dorking with the composer and his family, copying parts of a work for strings, a piece he based on some music of Thomas Tallis.

She also completed copying a solo violin piece for him. Peggy always claimed that Vaughan Williams borrowed a piece of music from her during this time. He apparently once said in good humour, 'One should always borrow from the little people; if you steal from the big people it shows.' Her retort had been, 'Good, then I shall borrow it back when I am a bigger person.' Peggy's Sinfonietta, which was her graduation piece when leaving the Royal College, contains exactly the same piece of music as Vaughan Williams' Fourth Symphony in F minor. Peggy pointed out that his piece, like hers, is notable for the dissonance on the second and seventh. 'It was a straight crib.' Peggy also claimed it was she who swung him away from his former folklore composition themes and into more modern twentieth-century music. In 1989 Peggy was to borrow parts of this same music back for her opera *Becket*.

Peggy's friends at the Royal College were a mixture of teachers and students. Along with Esther, they included Lennox Berkeley, Alan Rawsthorne, Franz Reizenstein, Gordon Jacob, Charles Kitson, Gustav Holst, John Ireland, Stanley Bate, and in her later years, another woman composer, Elisabeth Lutyens. All of these were to enjoy fame in one form or another later in their lives.

Sir Lennox Berkeley became one of England's most distinguished composers and a professor at the Royal Academy from the late 1940s until well into the 1960s. In 1989, while hunting down former student colleagues of Peggy's, I discovered that Sir Lennox Berkeley was still living in London. Ill health prevented him from being interviewed but his wife recalled for me some of the dialogue that she had heard told by Sir Lennox, then Lenny to his friends. She said, 'Lennox complained to Peggy of the classes they attended saying, "Everyone here sounds the same, except for Stanley Bate and yourself". Peggy sycophantically defended Vaughan Williams as a teacher.' Lennox had apparently been a questioning student and although he did not always have the agreement of his fellow students, his views were listened to seriously.

Alan Rawsthorne was later awarded the CBE for his contribution to music as a composer. Franz Reizenstein became a teacher in London at the Royal Academy of Music. Esther Rofe managed to earn a living back in Melbourne working for radio. Gordon Jacob was also awarded a CBE and, after a productive life of composition, rejoined the Royal College as a teacher until his retirement in 1966. Gustav Holst, a lifelong friend of Vaughan Williams who had studied with him at the college as a student, taught at the Royal College from 1919 to 1923 and was a guest lecturer and friend to Peggy during her attendance. John Ireland had been a teacher of Benjamin Britten's at the Royal College and also made guest appearances during Peggy's period. He too socialised with the Royal College students and staff. Elisabeth Lutyens became quite a distinguished composer and formed the Composers' Concourse in the 1950s. She too established her own publishing company, Olivan Press. She also received a CBE.

Stanley Bate, who was neck and neck in the talent stakes with Benjamin Britten, died too young to reach his full potential. He did, however, snare the heart of Peggy Glanville-Hicks for a good ten years.

Peggy's social world changed dramatically during her second and third years at college. Indira had returned to India, and Esther had indicated by letter her decision to remain in Australia. Her time and affection were now directed back to her friend and fellow student Stanley Bate. As well as being one of the more talented students, Peggy described him as 'beautiful to look at', and was impressed by his ability to stretch two notes past the octave on the piano. She teased him to write music that would exploit this unique physical ability. Stanley had written an opera at age seventeen which had been produced in Plymouth, and the proceeds donated to the relatives of people who had lost their lives in tragic accidents in the region. This noble gesture had endeared him to Peggy. She remarked that his family and hers both had roots in Cornwall—grandparents in both of their families had lived there. She was always pleased by any similarities to herself and looked for them in all her friends.

At twenty-four the young English composer was blond, had large grey eyes, a pale complexion and a cheeky smile. He amused Peggy with stories of family scandal. He said that his mother was really of Spanish origin, 'from the Spanish Armada. My ancestors invaded the decadent English.' He claimed: 'My grandfather, mother's side, boiled down the family silver to make me some stirrups for my horseriding. As you can imagine my father was horrified!'[8] Peggy was shocked and enchanted that such a refined English gentleman would dare to expose his own origins to criticism. Stanley pooh-poohed such formality and loved to raise an eyebrow or two just for the hell of it. Always in debt, he liked to live extravagantly, exhausting allowances and scholarships and any other money given him. But his good humour and talent made him a fashionable and much sought-after friend among the students at the Royal College of Music.

Peggy met Stanley's mother in what she described as a sordid house in Plymouth. While Peggy observed that the mother may have had some Spanish blood in her, she ascribed Stanley's rebelliousness to his mother's disdain for English puritanism. Bate's mother appeared, at the time, to be living separately from his father in modest surroundings. Peggy was unable to discover whether his mother ran away from her husband on a regular basis for dramatic effect, or whether in fact she had permanently separated from him. Stanley laughed about his mother's behaviour, his mother laughed, and there was never any clarity. Peggy accepted this and was in no doubt that Stanley had been given the finest upbringing and education. Perhaps, like his mother, he had a tendency to dramatise his life.

Peggy would have found Bate swashbuckling and attract-ive. She herself had a growing tendency towards grandiosity. She was mesmerised by Bate and found numerous excuses to be in his company. Not that this was difficult, as most of the popular students, herself included, socialised together at the local cafes and bars. A favourite haunt was the Cheshire Cheese, where Britten had taken her earlier. This ancient little pub in the middle of the city was almost Spanish in design, with a combination of early English architecture added. From outside it appeared a gloomy little den; inside it sparkled with laughter and noisy conversation, especially when the student crowd arrived.

One evening Peggy, Stanley and their college maestro, Sir Thomas Beecham, arrived for drinks at the Cheshire Cheese after a concert. Sir Thomas (whose family owned the well-known pharmaceutical company) became famous for his reputation as an expressive, extrovert, and witty conductor. The two students were in awe of him. On arriving at the Cheshire Cheese Sir Thomas hailed a taxi, deposited his coat and briefcase, sent the cab home ahead of himself and then proceeded to join them at the bar. The three held great conversation for the rest of the evening and then, having drunk more than a respectable amount, sauntered along the Strand in clumsy merriment. Peggy later recalled a jubilant Stanley inciting the noble Sir Thomas to join with him, raising his glass, in rejection of English puritanism. Mistakenly or mischievously they had brought the hotel glasses with them!

The arrival of Myrtle Glanville-Hicks at the end of this whirlwind year was cause for great excitement. Peggy had organised dinners and gatherings in the hope of introducing her mother to her friends. Myrtle was pleased to spend time with her daughter but, unfortunately for Peggy, had other plans. These included a six month tour of Europe visiting old friends and relatives. She had even brought a female companion along for the journey. To Peggy's surprise she arrived with a baby grand piano for her twenty-first birthday.

The news from home was that Peggy's father Ernest Glanville-Hicks, 'Glans' as his children affectionately called him, had been newly appointed to the Lord Mayor's Fund in Melbourne, a position he was to hold for twenty-five years.

He had also published a second anthology of poetry, titled *Turn of the Tide*.

Myrtle's visit brought back Peggy's homesickness for Australia and the family life she had almost forgotten. As her mother's departure drew near Peggy became quite depressed. They had done the usual tourist things, Covent Garden, the cathedrals, a trip up the Thames to visit Kew Gardens, a theatre visit or two. Mostly these activities had been shared with other companions. There had been little chance to talk. What could a young woman say to her mother? That she missed the attentions of childhood? That she didn't feel as if her mother had really come to visit her at all? That her life had changed dramatically and she wanted to explain it all to her? That she had a crush on Stanley Bate? Or that she simply wanted to shelter in the comfort of the familiar? The college workload was all-consuming and the rumours of war hurried her in her ambitions. She converted her sadness into work and threw herself into her musical studies with gusto.

The day her mother set sail for Europe, it seemed to her that everyone was passing in and out of her life at great speed. That night she cried out of loneliness because at twenty-one she was no longer a child.

NOTES

1. *The Australian Musical News*, Oct. 1932.
2. Royal College of Music library records, London.
3. Royal College of Music, prospectus records of 1931–32.
4. Royal College of Music library records.
5. 'Music Reviewed' by Virgil Thomson, *New York Herald–Tribune*, Jan. 1942.
6. Royal College of Music, library records.
7. James Melon Interview, State Library of Victoria, 18 Feb. 1980.
8. Interview with Peggy Glanville-Hicks, who recalled his exact words.

THE BAKERY

Peggy wanted to prove herself. She recognised that the ensuing years were of tremendous importance to her as a composer. One had to make the most of the opportunities the Royal College of Music gave, or depart with skills which for a woman meant that it amounted to little more than 'a stately finishing school'. She applied herself even more diligently during the final years of her study. The scholarship was always something to aim for and she knew if she failed to achieve anything short of excellence it would be taken from her and there would be only one place to go—home to Australia.

She was particularly inspired by her teacher Sir Malcolm Sargent, known as 'flash Harry' in music circles. Sargent coached her in conducting. He conducted the Royal Choral Society from 1928, and later conducted the Hallé Orchestra (1939–42), eventually settling with the BBC Symphony Orchestra in the 1950s.[1] Sir Thomas Beecham, the other British conductor with whom Peggy and Stanley Bate had shared a friendship, also had a profound influence on her learning during this period. Beecham would discuss with Peggy at length the importance of conducting and how it elevated the composition work. Peggy was impressed. Beecham agreed with her that conducting lacked female participation. Peggy was eager, but her first love was composition.

It was during her final years at college that Stanley Bate started to feature as more than a friend in Peggy's imagination. Peggy thought of him as a great pianist, a great composer, and noticed for the second time the softness of his hands. The time the two spent together grew more frequent. Both applied for the Octavia Travelling Scholarship along with many other students in the hope of advancing their careers as composers. The winners were announced at a recital given in the college music hall. Miraculously the two tied. Both

Stanley Bate and Peggy Glanville-Hicks would be funded to travel and study for a period of two years with the teacher or musical school of their choice. A silence fell over the students. Peggy cast a furtive glance at Stanley, who was already grinning at her. Sir Thomas Beecham reached across to Peggy and kissed her on the cheek. Applause broke out across the hall. Stanley made his way through the crowd, shaking hands and accepting congratulations. Upon reaching Peggy he hesitated. He hugged her tightly, stared cheekily at her and moved to kiss her. He stopped short and the two fell to laughter. It was a wonderful moment for them both. It meant a serious beginning for them both in the real world of composition.

In 1935, the Melbourne *Sun* carried an article entitled: 'Melbourne Girl Wins Rich Musical Prize'.[2] The article included quotes from the composer Ralph Vaughan Williams stating that, in his opinion, Miss Glanville-Hicks would eventually be responsible for compositions of great worth. Cyril Scott was quoted in praise of the songs of Miss Glanville-Hicks. He recounted the previous year's BBC Empire Broadcast of the young composer's work. The article closed with an explanation of the prize winner's plans: she would leave London for the continent the following October.

The scholarship was a rare distinction. In her application she had submitted a number of compositions including her opera *Caedmon*, a choral pastorale, the ballet *Hylas and the Nymphs*, and a piece known as *Spanish Suite*—a work in five movements that she had composed after a holiday in Spain. She also submitted a collection of music she had written for film.

Fired with enthusiasm, she set about locating two great teachers with whom she might like to study. This was not an easy task. It depended not only on the teacher's availability but also on his or her willingness to take the student. A number of composers were not interested in taking on a female composer, believing there was little chance of success for a woman. Peggy even went so far as to say that many great composers doubted the skill of a woman. She felt that male teachers saw real possibilities in the young male protégé, but doubted that a woman could distinguish herself or them in quite the same way. Unperturbed, Peggy wrote to several teachers at once. Nadia Boulanger, the famous French teacher, and the only woman she approached, declined to offer Peggy anything. So did most of the others. Finally she was accepted by Egon Wellesz in Vienna.

Egon Wellesz was not really the instructor she had hoped for. Wellesz had been a pupil of Schoenberg and was better known for surrealism, a method of composition based on the serial ordering of pitches.[3] The classical form of surrealism is dodecaphony, or twelve-tone compositions. That is to say the twelve notes of the chromatic scale recur in a predetermined order known as 'series'. Peggy had been informed that there would be discussion about atonal music in Vienna. (Atonality referred to the system of composing music in which no key is used.) Peggy was grateful if not enthusiastic when she was accepted. 'I don't like atonal music unless it is twentieth-century,' she said, 'but one ought not leave a stone unturned so I'll go.'

She enrolled with Wellesz in a course of musicology and advanced composition but lasted only two and a half months before leaving. She felt he repeated himself and that after such a glamorous and inspiring education at the Royal College of Music he had little to teach her. On her failure to complete the course, she commented to friends: 'I wrote two noisy sonatas in the serial technique and then tore them up on the way back to Paris on the train. I didn't want to become a twelve-tone rower, it just wasn't me.'

Disappointed and depressed, she arrived in Paris to face a gloomy winter. She organised accommodation in a cheap *pension* and settled down to take stock of her situation. On the train journey back to Paris she had decided to pursue Nadia Boulanger in the hope that she would reconsider, and accept her for study. Nadia Boulanger's sister Lili had been a composer and this proved to be the reason for her rejection of Peggy. Boulanger believed the path for her sister as a composer had been too difficult. Lili's life had been short and hellish and Boulanger saw no point in encouraging women further. She had lost faith in equality.

In Paris, Peggy learned that some of her colleagues from the Royal College of Music, including Lennox Berkeley, had recently left the studio of Nadia Boulanger. David Diamond was still studying with her, and two American composers had recently arrived. They were Leonard Bernstein and Samuel Barber. Peggy was optimistic that a discussion with Boulanger might prove fruitful. She began a series of letters to the famous teacher and on one occasion even managed to get herself invited to a salon party. Without a formal introduction she offered Boulanger her opinions on women and art. She said, 'A woman's creative years are also the years she is most capable of producing children. This is an enormous problem for her. While I recognise the dilemma, I only want to give birth to operas.' Boulanger was thoughtful and pleased by the unconventional Australian. Peggy left the party without declaring herself.

In New York, in 1989, Leonard Bernstein referred to the occasion. 'Nadia found satisfaction in her discussions with Peggy that night. She liked Peggy's intelligent mind. They shared a mutual admiration for Stravinsky, Debussy and Ravel. Peggy described Boulanger as having a young man's hands, yet beautiful and dynamic. It was the working methods of Boulanger that Peggy most admired but she was careful to appear light on this first encounter. We talked about it a day or so later in a cafe, Peggy and I. I couldn't understand Nadia's reluctance.'

Full of hope from her initial meeting, Peggy arrived at Boulanger's door the following week. Still the teacher was reluctant to take her on. Boulanger explained curtly that composing was no career for a woman. Peggy went away extremely disappointed. At the door she had reminded Boulanger of her sister's success. Lili Boulanger, who had died in 1918 aged twenty-five, had been the first woman composer to win the Prix de Rome. It was awarded in 1913 for her composition *Faust et Hélène*. Boulanger was adamant, and turned Peggy away. When she returned home to her little room at the *pension* she wrote yet another letter to Boulanger. This time she was angry and insulting. She reaffirmed her desire to learn, setting aside all efforts of intellectual persuasion. The weeks passed and this letter and several others went unanswered until quite unexpectedly one morning a telegram arrived for Peggy. It read: 'I am very busy. I have very little time. I see you are determined. Come at eleven p.m. This is the only free time I have. Nadia Boulanger.'

And so the lessons began. The first lasted just two hours, from eleven p.m. to one a.m. Peggy arrived that evening on the front doorstep of Boulanger's house clutching her scores under her arm and shivering. There was no light on inside but after a short while Boulanger appeared and greeted Peggy nonchalantly. The lesson was conducted in the normal fashion and Boulanger never once brought up the subject of her initial rejection. Peggy's studies with her were to last for just over a year and Boulanger was always encouraging and professional.

Nadia Boulanger had been discovered by the Americans around 1921 when composers Aaron Copland, Virgil Thomson and Melville Smith returned to New York full of praise for her. She conducted private lessons for a musical elite on the fourth floor of a standard French apartment block.[4] She taught piano playing, sight-reading, harmony, counterpoint, fugue, orchestration, analysis and composition. Her history was impressive. At the age of just thirty-four, she had held professorships at the French Conservatoire, at the École Normale de Musique, and at the American Conservatory in Fontainebleau. The American Conservatory was where the Americans first recognised her talents. A number of musicians and composers who later claimed to have been pupils of Boulanger in fact attended one of these institutions. It was only an elite who had the good fortune to be private students of the maestro and many hankered after such a rite of passage.

Boulanger's devotion as a teacher was unflagging, her working hours extensive. She took her first student as early as seven in the morning and her latest as late as midnight. She insisted that musical training without rigour, a word she liked to use, could be of no value. She believed every composer should also be a musician and that every musician, at least in training, a composer.

She herself played second organ at the church of the Madeleine on a regular basis and led a rigorous working life. She was active on a number of committees such as the Concerts Colonne, the second-oldest orchestra in Paris, and the Société Musicale Indépendante, the most advanced of modern music groups at the time. On Wednesday afternoons when she could have taken time off for herself, she invited her students to the apartment. There she played and analysed the most modern scores available: Stravinsky, Schoenberg and Mahler. Sometimes rare madrigals from the Renaissance would turn up, or works by Monteverdi, Luca Marenzio, or Gesualdo di Venosa. These were especially appreciated, and everyone would join in. The session ended after Boulanger's mother appeared with hot tea and cakes. Everyone knew that their departure was expected promptly after tea.[5]

Boulanger must have seemed a mysterious figure to her pupils. Her apartment was furnished in turn-of-the-century style, and sitting on each of the mantelpieces were framed mementoes of her father and her sister, Lili. Her father had been a professor at the Conservatoire. Lili was photographed taking her bow on winning the Prix de Rome. Following Lili's death Nadia dressed in mourning, with her brown hair tied into a neat bun. Each year Boulanger held a memorial for Lili. Nadia never married nor was she known to have any sort of romantic life. For the thirty years or so following her sister's death she looked after her sick and ageing mother.[6] She had many friends and colleagues who, with her work, seemed to complete her life.

Although she was well respected in France, only one French composer of international standing was a private pupil. This was Jean Françaix. Her influence was much greater on American musicians and composers. Among Peggy's contemporaries in this select circle were: David Diamond, Paul Bowles, Virgil Thomson, Aaron Copland, and Lennox Berkeley. It was rumoured that Boulanger had refused to teach George Gershwin on the grounds that rigorous musicianship might impede his natural flow of melody. She explained that 'unaccustomed musical exercise should not be added to the labour of creation'. Yet she always emphasised to her students the need to practise before composing. She insisted that the creative act should always be free, a gratuitous communication.[7]

America, she is supposed to have said, reminded her of the Russia of the 1840s, 'bursting with inspiration but poorly trained'. Her mother, referred to as a princess, was Russian. Nadia spoke fluent Russian and had a keen interest in observing music practices in countries experiencing political change. Her travel to corners of Europe's Eastern Bloc unnerved a few critics on occasions, but she displayed no trace of communistic tendencies which might perhaps have ended her brilliant career with American students.

According to American music critic Virgil Thomson, it was Boulanger's critical acumen that distinguished her as a teacher. She could understand at sight almost any piece of music: its meaning, its nature, its motivation, its unique existence, and she could reflect back to her students like a mirror.[8] Peggy's opinion of her teaching supports this view: 'She would wait two or three weeks when you started lessons with her to see what your natural directions were. Then she would teach you to realise them. There are many major musicians and composers but there was only one Nadia Boulanger!'

On her seventy-fifth birthday Boulanger was conducting the New York Philharmonic in four concerts. She had, on other occasions, conducted the Boston Symphony Orchestra, the Philadelphia Orchestra, London's Royal Philharmonic Orchestra, as well as the best Parisian orchestras. She also taught at Harvard. She died in 1979 aged ninety-two.

While Peggy was studying under Boulanger she continued corresponding with Stanley. He had chosen to study under Hindemith in Berlin but his long letters were full of complaints. He claimed Hindemith was trying to clone all of his pupils, and that he was dictatorial. Stanley exaggerated, as was his nature, but Peggy never doubted him. He complained that Benjamin Britten had usurped him in London, and had knocked him out of the race. While it was true that Bate had a promising career ahead of him, his view of Britten cannot be substantiated. He probably harboured some jealousy, especially as he knew the place Britten had once held in Peggy's heart. Peggy sympathised with Bate, further validating his complaints. She wrote him sympathetic letters which began 'Dear Foxkin', a pet name for him which related to his appearance. He had rather long hair for the period, and a smile that was full of pearly teeth. Most of Peggy's letters were aimed at cheering him up. She also wrote to him about her theories on neo-classicism. 'It is rather like taking an old brownstone house and putting a snappy glass and nickel frontage on it. The same old house stands inside, beautifully camouflaged.' Later Peggy wrote whole chapters for magazines which explained the development of music in architectural terms, thus making it accessible to the layperson. A favourite phrase was 'Architecture is frozen music.'

Stranded in Berlin, Stanley Bate became jealous of Peggy's study with Boulanger while he battled on with Hindemith. He was aware that every notable American composer was passing through Boulanger's rooms. He could see that Peggy was bursting with musical ideas and directions and fast becoming part of a very influential set as American composers continued to arrive in Paris. Indicating some exasperation with his jealousy, she wrote: 'I am of the new world and you are of the old and frankly it is beginning to show.' Bate was enraged with her arrogance. Her letters ceased for some time; his did not.

Nadia Boulanger challenged Peggy head-on, teaching her

technique and yet helping her to uncover her own style and inclinations. For the first time Peggy began to feel a stirring of something completely original within herself. No longer in the shade and colour of her former teachers, she began to create for the first time. At twenty-four she felt herself to be at the centre of the musical world. After some time of not corresponding she finally wrote a one-line letter to Bate: 'Dear Foxkin, Neo-classicism is the only canal to swim in and all the Americans are doing just that.' Bate was overjoyed that she had corresponded and began writing more frequently.

Peggy still nurtured an affection for Bate. In her little *pension* in Paris she would scratch down notes in her journal and tear them out for inclusion in her letters to him. She spoke of obliterating the diatonic system, of her love of Indian music, of modal scales that fell between the influences of the West and the East. In one letter to Bate she described with wit the size of her room. She would perch herself on the top of the piano to work. The piano took up almost the entire floor leaving just enough space for a single bed and a gas burner stove and sink. With a pencil in her mouth she would hurriedly write down her thoughts and then leap down on to the piano stool, practising what she described as a type of mental levitation. She would even call out sometimes, 'Harmony, throw it away' (elaborating on her serious view was that harmony was redundant in modern music), and all her papers and music sheets would be strewn down from the top of the piano. To all of these tales Stanley responded. Most of Peggy's humour and exuberance was private and Bate alone had a window into her secret life. Despite all the important colleagues she met, she felt alone in Paris, composing by day, attending classes with Boulanger by night.

During her time under the direction of Nadia Boulanger Peggy produced a series of works. These included: Prelude and Scherzo for Large Orchestra, Concerto for Flute and Small Orchestra, Choral Suite (five movements) for Women's

Voices, Oboe and Strings, and a string quartet. She also produced a pastorale for women's chorus and cor anglais and Suite for String Orchestra with Oboe. This was quite an achievement for one year's study.

During her year in Paris in 1936 Peggy realised the true direction of her future works. She would proceed from neo-classicism, taking what she needed from her training, and incorporating elements of Indian, Greek or Asian musical structures. These she would synthesise into a flavour peculiarly her own which she referred to, using her initials, as the P. G.-H. style. Her musical creations were not contrived but prompted by heart and mind. Her inspiration came from within. She heard strange unwritten sounds in her dreams, and in her humming while she did the morning dishes. All she had to do was to find the context, to seal it, as if in a glass chamber, for all to hear.

Peggy managed to stretch out her scholarship for a year and a half, but it was scarcely enough to keep her. Stanley, who had received the same amount of money, had spent his scholarship in just three months. In his letters he indicated that he was making plans to visit Peggy in Paris to study with Boulanger himself.

In May 1938, the International Society for Contemporary Music held its annual festival in London. This festival, found-ed in 1922, was specific in its choice of 'new music'. It claimed to be a festival for the advancement of contemporary music. It attracted the leading critics and authorities from Europe, England and America. Eminent musicians and composers sought inclusion in the festival program. It was held annually in a range of leading music centres around the world.

Peggy was the first Australian composer to be represented in the festival. Her contribution included two movements from her Choral Suite which were conducted by Adrian Boult. These pieces had a lilting quality, a distant unseizable mood. They were technically clever, probably a deciding factor in their inclusion. Boult was an exceptional conductor and an asset to Peggy's music.

But the festival didn't get off to a very good start. Litigation threatened the Russian Ballet's opening night at Covent Garden, a dispute having arisen between impresarios as to who owned the rights to certain ballets of the repertoire. Despite court orders and the possibility of litigation, the season opened on time. Peggy's picture appeared in some of the associated newspaper clippings. She is featured smiling underneath a rather oddly-shaped felt hat, a pretty face to distract readers from the contentious issues surrounding the festival's opening. Despite all the difficulties, the program proceeded more or less as planned. Some performances were rescheduled and one or two replaced at the last hour.

Peggy appeared on the same program as Lennox Berkeley, Samuel Barber, Alan Bush and Franz Reizenstein. Their works were recorded and featured in a broadcast to Australia on national relay, reaching Peggy's proud family and friends. Margaret Sutherland played a piece from Peggy's music live to air as part of a special accompanying feature. An article which appeared in the Melbourne *Age* listed the festival participants, which included Joaquín Nin-Culmell (brother of Peggy's friend Anaïs Nin), and commented on Peggy's contribution and her two Choral Songs for Women's Voices. It was said to have 'pleased its audiences by its clear sounding use of the medium which its composer had cleverly employed, and its constant appeal as something well said, and easily assimilated'.[9] Also highlighted in the program were the works of Bartók, Křenek, Copland, Hindemith and the ever popular young British composer Benjamin Britten.

The two other women composers who appeared at the festival were Gitta Bartók from Hungary and Viteslava Kapralova from Czechoslovakia. Sadly their work was not discussed in the article. The women appeared in photographs but all the text was devoted to the male participants. The titles of the women's works were also omitted from the article. The photograph of Peggy, appearing beside these women, shows a peaky young frightened girl with dark eyes, dark wavy hair parted on the side and a necklace of large white pearls.[10] The Melbourne *Sun* also mentioned the festival. 'Year by year,' an unidentified journalist wrote, 'a galaxy of talent emerges and is forced to move abroad if they are to win wide recognition.' The article hints repeatedly at the lack of support for artists in Australia.

Peggy's contribution as an Australian made musical history, as well as representing a major advance for her as a composer. The performance of the Choral Suite she remembered only because of a silly incident. She had arrived at the final rehearsal, trimly dressed in a check suit highlighted with a red spotted bow tie. She found Sir Adrian Boult, who was conducting the orchestra for the performance, wearing the male replica of her outfit. 'But Sir Adrian was a gentleman. He didn't say a word!' She laughed during the retelling of this story because of the pleasure she took in twinship, an oddity that seemed to recur throughout her life.

It was about this time that Peggy decided that her name was too trivial for her vocation. She felt it disadvantaged her to announce her gender on programs and so she asked to be billed as P.G.-H. or P. Glanville-Hicks. She believed a bias was in place where female composers were concerned, and preferred anonymity. From this point on she always signed her compositions in one of these genderless forms.

NOTES

1. A. Isaacs and E. Martin, *Dictionary of Music*, Hamlyn Publishing Group, United Kingdom, 1982, p. 348.
2. Melbourne *Sun*, 26 June 1935.
3. *Dictionary of Music*.
4. *A Virgil Thomson Reader*, Houghton Mifflin Group, United States, 1981, pp. 52–56.
5. Ibid.
6. Ibid.
7. 'Greatest Music Teacher', *New York Times* magazine, 4 Feb. 1962.
8. *A Virgil Thomson Reader*.
9. Melbourne *Age*, 16 July 1938.
10. Richard Capell, *Daily Telegraph*, 18 June 1938.

THE
COMPOSER'S WIFE

When Stanley Bate arrived in Paris, Peggy had planned to be pleasantly distant. But the inevitable conversations, the outings, the concerts and then the mutual love of music deepened the relationship that had begun in London. Stanley joined the music circles that had for so long been known to him only through Peggy's letters. Mixing with the American composers, Stanley and Peggy became entranced with the possibility of a future visit to the United States. In the meantime Stanley felt he should develop his reputation in London so, after a short stint of studying with Boulanger and late nights spent talking with Peggy, the two young composers decided to return to England. There they shared a house together until friends and colleagues began to gossip. Everyone seemed to think it rather sinful that a man and woman should live together under the same roof without the respectability of marriage. And so, in 1938, Peggy Glanville-Hicks and Stanley Bate were married in the Kensington Registry Office at eleven a.m. The brief ceremony was witnessed by two fellow students and the couple moved into a rented apartment in Camden Hill.

The two honeymooned in a tiny town called Foumex in the Swiss Alps. Stanley was desperate to find a piano as soon as they arrived. In a fit of inspiration he walked the length of the village and made enquiries. The only piano in the entire village belonged to a cobbler. Stanley described it to a journalist:

> It was a frightful old box of fretwork with jangly strings, but it had all the notes and it served. On top of the piano were framed portraits of five generations of cobblers and they

used to jump around and rattle when I played—in anger no doubt. There were also some glass covered wax figures and these they moved out, probably for safety. All during my composing the cobbler banged at his last, and I sort of got some of the rhythm of his pounding into my first movement. The cobbler was a good fellow but I had a feeling he didn't like my music. No yodel in it.[1]

Oddly enough, some years later when Concerto for Piano and Orchestra, written by Bate in Foumex, was performed in Carnegie Hall by Bruno Walter and the Philharmonic, Douglas Gilbert, a *World Telegram* staff writer, described the piece, as 'a musical adaptation of a cobbler lamming his last'.

Initially, life in London had a settling effect on Peggy. Old friends from the Royal College of Music soon regrouped. Lennox Berkeley, Alan Rawsthorne and others all came to visit. Elisabeth Lutyens visited Peggy with her four children. Like Peggy, Liz, as Peggy knew her, retained her maiden name. She was the daughter of the architect Sir Edwin Lutyens and she and Peggy liked to discuss design and form. Elisabeth also wrote articles for publication, another similarity the two women shared. At this time Elisabeth was already becoming a major name in music circles.

The apartment rented by the couple was chosen for musical rather than domestic needs. It was at the top of an old house at Camden Hill with a panoramic view over the city's rooftops. Essentially the space consisted of two large studio areas. Peggy described her husband's studio as black and white, with a very modern black patent leather couch from Finland, padded doors, a white hair rug carpet, dead white walls and a huge black piano placed strategically at the centre. Her own studio, which was above his on the next floor, was decorated in brown and cream, her favourite colours. The furniture was white wrought iron. Her small brown piano stood inconspicuously in the corner.

The arrival of the two pianos had caused quite a ruckus in the neighbourhood. Neighbours gathered downstairs outside the apartment with theories about how the pianos could be levered through the doors. Peggy shrieked when cutting the legs off her baby grand was suggested. Finally some ropes and pulleys were produced so the pianos could be juggled up the stairwell. This failed and the pianos were hoisted up three floors and the upstairs windows removed.

Predictably, the domestic quarter of the apartment was on the same floor as Peggy's. It consisted of a toilet and basin, a minute kitchen, one small shelf and a smallish bath near the stove. Alterations were necessary but the cost of amenities took second place to the studio requirements. For a time they bought household things for their apartment and were happy enough. A sofa bed, an armchair or two and an unusual ceramic heater. They painted and decorated, enjoying the process of making a home together.

All was well except for what Stanley called the 'piano problem', meaning the noise they both made while composing. Stanley had various commissions to honour. Peggy was expected to wash the dishes and maintain the smooth running of the house. Financial responsibilities also fell to Peggy. Although Stanley had commissions, he was paid only intermittently and he spent most of it on outings, suits and friends. Peggy slowed down her own composition output and instead began copying work for other composers, including Stanley. This and some freelance journalism made up the bulk of her financial contribution. The weekly bills were managed and paid for by Peggy, while Stanley worked on unhindered. The Bates hired a housekeeper on their small income as was customary for the English of Stanley's background. Her name appealed to Peggy and was a deciding factor in her employment. Horaca Bundle came to clean twice a week.

Stanley had drinking binges, which often followed the completion of a work, and these sometimes resulted in prison detention. A call would come late at night: 'Peggy, I need fifty pounds to bail me out.'[2] Peggy would dutifully rise from her bed, gather her funds and retrieve him. She would make excuses for his behaviour. She sometimes even rationalised his homosexuality with claims that various policemen had framed him for withholding sexual favours. She bore this shame privately. Neither dramatic nor resentful, she shielded him and herself from discussion of his behaviour. Practical in nature, she adopted an attitude of 'live and let live'. Stanley was oblivious to the strain he placed her under. After such incidents he would grow nasty and complain whenever he heard Peggy playing in her studio. 'Our pianos can hear each other,' he would screech up the stairs.

Peggy eventually stopped writing music altogether during her marriage to Stanley. She concentrated all her energies on articles for publications such as *Harpers Bazaar* and *Vogue*, seeking only domestic and financial harmony. For one who had sought a musical career with such urgency and determination, who had travelled thousands of miles from home to achieve her goal, such acquiescence must have been painful.

Peggy liked to tell interviewers, 'I married him to keep him out of trouble rather than get him out of trouble.' She spoke in this manner quite soon after the marriage took place. Perhaps she thought it was obvious to strangers that she had a problem husband. His drunk and disorderly charges and his inability to manage money were not all she had to contend with. The bail money for homosexual charges was high. Perhaps Peggy had not realised fully the consequences of marrying Stanley or maybe she was naively optimistic. She was involved with the man she adored and in the early days of the marriage it appears there was some form of sexual relationship. This broke down within a very short time.

Peggy was also known to comment of Stanley: 'He is 110 per cent composer.' There is little doubt that the percentage in him that included their relationship was non-existent from the beginning. Despite this, the two initially settled into a union in London, confident that a career for both of them would be possible.

Stanley's work was being performed by orchestras for the BBC and at public concerts all over England. He had a piano concerto commissioned by Sir Henry Wood for the promenade season, and his second symphony was scheduled for presentation in the coming winter. This was interrupted by the advent of war.

Sir Henry decided to present the symphony when he had heard only the first movement, so impressed was he by Bate's talent. Stanley was also commissioned to do several compositions for the Princess De Polignac, who had taken a great interest in young composers, and he inscribed *Six Pieces for an Infant Prodigy* to her. Ralph Vaughan Williams was said to have commented to Peggy that he regarded Stanley as his successor, although Peggy may have invented this statement to pacify Stanley. Stanley was again becoming fiercely jealous of Benjamin Britten and seemed to be in constant need of reassurance.

War was declared and although no attacks took place initially, wartime procedures were followed methodically, with preparations for the worst. Peggy and Stanley's apartment was beside a water-tower. Like Kensington Palace and other key sites it was a constant source of worry because it was regarded as a target. A balloon barrage went up over the water-tower. There were dozens of canvas balloons filled with gas appearing all over London. Peggy and Stanley were instructed, along with their neighbours, in the operation of the barrage. Peggy took her turn tethering and manoeuvring the balloon, telling friends at the time, 'If a gale blows up we'll all go sailing across London.' The rationale for this balloon precaution was that it would prevent the Germans from getting close enough to be effective.

Even Stanley took his turn manning a barrage, but he complained constantly, and was known to make derogatory comments about the limitations of England's aircraft capability. This made for poor relations with the neighbours. The Bates' commitment to music was of no interest for other workers. Stanley was not in the armed forces, a fact which made local people irritated and disrespectful. He had been spared from enlistment because of a leg injury from a truck accident years earlier. He did limp on occasions, although

Peggy thought his beauty alone could well have been a deterrent for any heterosexual admissions officer.

The musical careers that had started out so well were beginning to look grim. Some years later Peggy told a Melbourne newspaper: 'When the war broke out and all organised music in London collapsed, my husband and two others organised Les Ballets Trois Arts, a company which kept dancers and a large theatre staff in employment.' This group also consisted of former colleagues from the Royal College of Music and other musician friends. Stanley arranged concerts at blackout prices, beginning with his own works, presented by the Wessex Philharmonic Orchestra.

With Tony Delrenzio, a young Italian composer well known among the moderns, he also wrote music for the ballet *Perseus*, which was presented at the Lyric Theatre, Hammersmith, and later at the Arts Theatre, Leicester Square. The piece was designed by Pamela Boden, who was already exhibiting successfully in Paris. Despite the war, the production was well attended. Elisabeth Lutyens, who like some of the other composers found a niche for herself in film and radio during the war, also assisted with the company.

London was geared up for war. Operations became more sophisticated and daily the papers increased the state of anxiety. During the evenings all houses drew their blinds. Lighting was kept to a minimum and despite the nightly roar of air-raid sirens, air-raid shelters were in short supply. During blackouts many people gathered up their bedding and made for underground stations to sleep in safety for the night. Families could be seen huddled together reading bedtime stories, adjusting pillows and pouring hot coffee from a thermos. Children could be heard crying over the hum of talk.

Peggy, Stanley, Elisabeth Lutyens and a few other Royal College of Music graduates decided to perform concerts in the underground. They would join the underground train in East Dulwich and progress to Ealing, giving a thirty minute concert at each station, and sometimes more when the trains stopped in between. Choosing only twentieth-century 'contemporary music', as Peggy called it, they soothed the nerves of the air-raid dwellers with Satie, Debussy and a variety of scores from the new work of Glanville-Hicks, Bate, Lutyens, Berkeley and any other composer present or favoured for promotion at the time. Stanley would drag the drums and instruments in, chatting to the train driver at each stop, Sometimes he even sang. He had a light baritone voice which Peggy had not heard before their marriage. The group would leave each station with cheering crowds and applause. Some of the people would pat them on the back as they left or shake hands thoughtfully. The seriousness of the war situation was conveyed in a glance.

Stanley's exclusion from the army was both a relief and a liability. Handsome and fit-looking, he continually encountered resentment for his failure to enlist. He regarded his concerts and station entertainment as his contribution to the war effort. As the war intensified the first signs of an increasingly fragile mental state began to show. He returned from a visit to the doctor to tell Peggy he was suffering nervous tension and the doctor had suggested he take a complete rest. Peggy nursed him back to health and this mini-breakdown passed.

Pamela Henn-Colin, head of the Arts Council in London, advised Peggy and Stanley to return to Australia to further their musical careers. London was in chaos, with standing room only, and Peggy was an Australian citizen. It was obvious that her choices were limited in Britain, so she decided to follow Henn-Colin's advice. Without telling Stanley, she wrote letters to Australian conductors seeking work on his behalf, in the hope of persuading him to accompany her home. When Stanley was invited to play a concerto with conductor Sir Bernard Heinze and the Melbourne Symphony Orchestra, he accepted immediately.

The couple took a ship bound for Australia, sailing from Southampton near the end of 1940. The ship, *Strathallan*, stopped at Gibraltar, Bombay, Perth, Adelaide and finally after six weeks, Melbourne. It was an ordinary passenger liner, much like the one Peggy had left Australia on ten years before. Bedding consisted of bunks with the standard grey army blankets that were so familiar to Australian households.

The sea was often rough; Peggy and Stanley would find themselves reading books most of the night to ward off nausea. Bass Strait proved to be the most treacherous and Stanley spent one entire night vomiting on deck. The other passengers were friendly and on calm nights Stanley organised sing-songs to pass the time. He kept his captive audience enthralled with songs he had written himself. His snappy English tailored suits gave the impression of an entertainer, and when he spoke his rich English accent made him all the more attractive. Although his drinking on board was often beyond an acceptable level, his appearance and musical talent made forgiveness easy.

Peggy's family was waiting by the dock to greet them on their arrival in Melbourne. Beric Glanville-Hicks, Peggy's younger brother, was very glad of Stanley's arrival. Not only did he find Stanley a polite and charming drinking companion in a house where liquor was rarely served, but he had a most impressive wardrobe. 'He was aesthetic looking, slightly precious,' said Beric, a second year medical student at the time, who borrowed a different jacket or suit every day. Stanley, according to Beric, had sixty suits, a mockery of Peggy's careful financial planning. Beric would arrive at med school in fashionable Harris tweeds with a beautifully lined overcoat, and create quite a stir among the student population. Luxury items such as English tailored suits had been in short supply since the Depression. Beric described Stanley as likeable, with long hair (it crept down to his collar), and a beautiful English accent. 'As for his homosexuality,' Beric said, 'I hadn't heard of it. I mean it wasn't a medical condition.'

Stanley was accepted into the Glanville-Hicks household in Hawthorn. According to Beric his parents passed little comment on their daughter's new husband, although Beric was convinced that, had they been truly pleased, it would have been apparent. It seemed to Beric that his sister had changed since leaving home. She now appeared more stylish in dress. Never one for frilly things, England had sculptured her so that she was almost unrecognisable from the girl who had left. Her voice had become more affected. Beric felt Bate had possibly married his sister for convenience. He detected a coolness which might have been an indifference towards Peggy. The dependency which Peggy spoke of was not immediately recognisable to the outside world. Beric was irritated by his sister's use of the name 'Foxkin' when addressing Bate. He believed she was impressed with Stanley's music, that this alone made her happy, more happy than he thought it should. It was already obvious to Beric that Peggy's composition work was taking second place to Stanley's career. Beric had seen his sister leave their family home passionate for a career in music. Now he saw a wife prepared to relinquish everything for marriage.

Stanley's plan when he came to Australia had been to take the ship on to San Francisco when the Melbourne job ended, spend some time in America and ultimately make his way back to England. He fretted for London almost as soon as he arrived. He needed London, and leaving it was always difficult. Peggy was glad to be home for a spell, although most of her connections with Melbourne friends had been broken in her long absence. She was keen none the less to show off her handsome young English husband.

As the secretary of the Lord Mayor's Fund, Peggy's father Ernest Glanville-Hicks was employed to raise the necessary funds for metropolitan hospitals and charities. There were society functions and gatherings to which Peggy and Stanley were invited because of her father's position. Myrtle Glanville-Hicks kept herself occupied gardening and reading. She was also an active member of the Rotary Club. Beric, still living at home, was recovering from the loss of his childhood sweetheart Nola Nicholas who, once a childhood friend of Peggy's, had lived next door. Instead of Beric, Nola had married Peggy's friend, the violinist Yehudi Menuhin, who had appeared on the scene offering all the charm and talent of the musical world.

'The Aspro family, the trade name of Nicholas, who imported and sold the aspirin drug,' Beric later told me.

They all had the most wonderful red hair! Nola, a beautiful girl, had the most coppery hair of them all. I played tennis with her brother, Lindsay. I holidayed with them at their property at Macedon on several occasions. Well, Yehudi married Nola and Yehudi's sister married Lindsay. Lindsay ended up someone's grandfather and the Nicholas family got very involved with the Menuhins. And I stayed single. For a while anyway.

Stanley was welcomed into the music circles of Melbourne and his participation noted in newspapers. Peggy became simply the composer's wife. Remarkably, this went unchallenged by friends or family. Perhaps they believed the loss of a career for a woman was normal. Peggy was still in love with her new husband, and his success and adjustment to her homeland was important to her. She wanted him to love Australia. But while he enjoyed giving a series of concerts, and being in the company of the Melbourne music set, he stilled yearned for change. When the war had broken out, many composers had left for the United States and Stanley was eager to get there. Peggy was also interested in America, but in the meantime work continued to arrive for Stanley.

At the end of their first year in Australia they moved from Melbourne to Sydney, where Stanley had been invited to work on a string and piano orchestral piece for the Sydney Symphony Orchestra. With no options open to her musically, Peggy decorated their small apartment in Potts Point and felt neglected. Newspaper stories appeared celebrating the husband and wife composer team, but there were no offers of work for her.

The marriage was beginning to show signs of strain. Peggy was lonely and possibly jealous of her husband's career and sexuality, both of which excluded her. She had lost her own career path and it wasn't enough to live for her husband's success, although a part of her still responded to this old cultural reflex. At a deep level she was discontented. The more success Bate had, the more he distanced himself from her, either to defend himself from her jealousy or out of selfishness. With success his drinking increased, and so did the number of his temper tantrums. There were domestic scenes. Bate was given to violent outbursts and Peggy bore the brunt of these in silence, perhaps believing herself responsible for provoking the tantrums. To avoid the problems at home she sought distractions, a path to follow. She attended performances in theatre and opera, and made contact where possible at social gatherings with directors and producers. She had succeeded in finding work opportunities for Stanley but was unable to find work for herself.

Composition being the profession it is, one cannot simply call up an arts administrator of an opera company and ask for a job composing. The subtle nature of the art requires that someone somewhere display interest in having you join them on a production. If Peggy had been too pushy she might have appeared vulgar, too direct or worse, in need of the money! She had her husband's reputation to consider now as well as her own, and this burdened her even more. Before the war, in London, she had been able to phone several organisations and plant an idea for a work which would ultimately include herself. The network was accessible and she was familiar with the protocol. In Sydney, most of the work Stanley was engaged in derived from word-of-mouth contacts. The sophisticated young composer impressed with his charm and was given the opportunity to display his skill. His appointments were usually in conjunction with the symphony orchestras of Sydney and Melbourne.

In 1936 the ABC had set up concert orchestras in all six capitals and begun annual subscription seasons of orchestral concerts. The Arts Council of Australia, known then as the Council for the Encouragement of Music and the Arts, was founded and became active in bringing the arts to country and provincial centres. The Arts Council had been founded under the leadership of an Australian singer Dorothy Helmrich, who herself had made a reputation abroad. Peggy thought that having a female as head might create opportunities for her. But there was no obvious female solidarity. Australia was in some ways more conservative concerning women artists and composers than other countries. According to Peggy, women writers were becoming acceptable only after it was discovered that Miles Franklin and Henry Handel Richardson were in fact women. Any favouritism between women applicants and senior women members of arts bodies was severely frowned upon. And no woman with power would consider it for fear of losing credibility with her male colleagues, despite the fact that cronyism had long been practised among men.

There was no-one to introduce or recommend Peggy for work and Stanley did not push his wife's case. She most certainly would not have asked him to. It appeared to Peggy at the time that the world of polite musical society was male, and that women composers were invisible or nonexistent. Margaret Sutherland was the only other woman who was composing in Australia, and she was not overly visible during Peggy's visit. It simply never occurred to anyone to give Peggy work. Articles had spoken of her talent. The Melbourne newspapers had celebrated her as 'a young and gifted composer' but nothing clicked. Stanley had only as much work behind him as his wife. They had tied in winning a scholarship from the Royal College of Music and Peggy had created good work while studying with Boulanger. Peggy concluded from dinner party conversations that in Australia men in positions of power did not negotiate a contract with a woman. She felt confined to the realm of novelty.

Stanley's homosexual affairs had begun again and his male flirtations were becoming obvious to friends. 'Stanley and I are a combination of pot luck and aristocracy,' Peggy would say. 'He is just too elegant, too beautiful, to have been born a man.' In this way she aligned herself with Stanley's male lovers and excused his infidelity. She seems to have needed to romanticise her situation, and idealise Stanley, though some newspaper reports recorded a strange rivalry in their relationship. The Melbourne *Age* reported:

> Even the least observant eye, meeting for the first time the visiting young English composer and his wife, Mr and Mrs Stanley Bate, would notice immediately that they are dressed in matching materials, and similar styles. 'My husband does not approve of my wearing mannish clothes,' admits Mrs Bate—who was Peggy Glanville-Hicks of Melbourne, before her marriage in London. 'He would prefer me to choose more feminine frocking, but, even for his sake I cannot change my style. I did give up, at his special request, wearing a man's felt hat, but I shall keep to tailor-mades, which I have always liked. I have costumes made in grey, navy pencil stripes and brown and fawn tweeds, the same materials as my husband has selected for suits. Still, notwithstanding our rivalry and the fact that Stanley always won the honours, we have managed to get along together!'[3]

The *ABC Weekly* also ran an article about them, entitled 'They Scorn Romanticism'. It depicted a smiling, homely couple in their flat at Potts Point. The journalist described 'Peggy's twenty-eight year old husband glancing across his table, littered with sheets of music to Peggy's table also littered with sheets of music [not hers] to observe in his wife an industrious composer, a muse and a rival in one.' The journalist questioned Bate on neo-classicism. 'Stravinsky is the greatest composer and Hindemith and Bartók,' Bate said. 'Against all these, you have Schoenberg, the last of the romantics; his atonalism has pushed romanticism as far as it can go. Neo-classicism is a return to clarity of form, a reaction against romanticism.'

Irritated by the journalist's lack of response, Bate accused him of not grasping the complexities he was alluding to. Peggy quietly present throughout had recognised Stanley's *faux pas* and interjected with praise for Australian orchestras. But Bate could not be saved and the journalist wrote: 'Bate denounces Australia as lacking any real audiences. He voices his despondency with the ABC and dismisses it in comparison to the more grandiose BBC.' Stanley had been drinking and his raving was evident. 'Hindemith is brilliant,' said Bate. 'He has written the only treatise on modern technique that is any good. He's the greatest German composer.' Bate had denounced the composer repeatedly during his training. The interview lost focus. Peggy attempted to save face by raising the topic of marriage. The journalist asked Bate, 'You met while studying?' 'Yes we did,' snapped Bate and closed off altogether.[4]

Peggy's recollection of this visit to Australia was as the negation of her musical ideas and aspirations. She was ignored as a composer except in title alone. Newspapers were interested in the clothes of Mrs Bate. The headlines reveal all:

'Mr and Mrs Stanley Bate looking over his work';

'Mrs Bate not as famous as her husband is also a composer';

'Mrs Stanley Bate whose brilliant work as a composer has earned a reputation, is an Australian.'[5]

In 1937, the *Sunday Sun & Guardian*, wrote: 'Mrs Bate's work for chorus and stringed instruments, conducted by Sir Adrian Boult.' Next line: 'Very slim and young looking, with dark hair brushed back from the face and piled in curls on top of her head, Mrs Bate has always loved music.' Absent from this particular article was the fact that this brief mention of her work related to an international event (the International Society for Contemporary Music Festival) at which Peggy was the first Australian composer ever to be represented.

In November 1940, the *Sunday Sun & Guardian* gossip column announced the arrival of Noël Coward at a major musical event accompanied by the Bates. Coward was described as brittle, disliking publicity but capable of wit and charm. Stanley was described as the distinguished composer and his work made mention of. Peggy was not mentioned.

Another rare article caught Peggy in full swing, claiming that a return to form was imminent in contemporary music. She discussed the modern romantic period.

'With all its wilful exaggerations and abuse of colour to the detriment of form it has been succeeded by a wave of neo-classicism. In Germany for example Hindemith has gone back to Bach. In England they have gone back to the Elizabethans.'

The interviewer in this instance capitalised on the dialogue of the composer and bothered to quote her, but failed to take up any of her provocative musical commentary. Instead, he completed the article with details of her physical appearance and dress. Peggy was stating quite emphatically that the romantic period had ended and not before time. She was also identifying herself as a composer with neo-classicist leanings. It was an open invitation for the interviewer to seek clarification and give her a chance to discuss her musical views. This did not happen. Her eloquence of speech and articulation of ideas made her an easy interviewee to quote; unfortunately her words were used to garnish rather than to clarify.[6]

If nothing else, Peggy's clothes certainly drew attention that month. The Melbourne *Age* wrote: 'Mr and Mrs Stanley Bate are rival composers who dress alike ... The fashion of women composers wearing mannish clothes was [also] noted at the BBC's concert. Mrs Bate in a long evening skirt, tunic cut to represent tails, lapels faced with ribbon and a white dickey of soft silk.' He went on, 'Mrs Bate, despite her preference for severely cut clothes is a charming slim young brunette with a boyish figure and a soft coiffure ot closely arranged curls all over her head.'[7]

Another Melbourne article titled 'Manly garb for musical women', of the same date, unwittingly captured Peggy's attitude to press commentary on women: 'I was interested in a Czech girl at the International Society for Contemporary Music, a composer,' Peggy said. 'She was dressed in a dinner jacket suit with a black bow tie.' This article missed Peggy's humour, and continued to exploit the same technique when describing Nadia Boulanger, also depicted with 'masculine flavour' (referring to her dress). She was ridiculed for the radical, masculine way she conducted the New York Philharmonic Orchestra by dispensing with the baton and conducting with her hands! Whether these women did dress in male clothing to make a point, to be visible, is difficult to know. It could merely have been cruel journalism that trivialised them as pseudo-men. Peggy believed that the newspapers only revealed the attitude society already held of women, that is, that only their clothing could be of interest.

A retrospective article in the *Herald* traced the events that led up to the couple's arrival in Sydney. Mention was made of the pioneering efforts of Bate in establishing entertainment during the blackouts in London. His wife, unnamed, was said to have busied herself with everything everyone else forgot— from running around the newspaper offices with publicity shots, to the supervision of lighting on location. This same article concluded by recapping Stanley's success in composition with the ABC orchestra, and then flippantly revealed that Bate had experienced a complete breakdown in London before being brought to Australia by his Australian wife.[8]

It was while they were still living in Potts Point that Stanley received an offer of work that was to have lasting repercussions for their marriage. This time the positon was at Harvard University and as always, without consulting Peggy, Bate accepted immediately. But Peggy was quite eager to leave Australia, and decided to base herself in New York where she hoped to pick up the pieces of her career. America, or at least New York, appealed as a more equal place for women. Stanley agreed to commute. He would move to Harvard and she to New York, and they would meet at weekends. As the relationship was strained, the temporary separation was a desirable arrangement.

Peggy and Stanley arrived in New York with fifteen pounds a piece. Stanley took up the position as guest lecturer at Harvard, but soon moved back to New York and Peggy. They took an apartment at 17 East 59th Street. The Bates, as they were referred to, lived on the top floor of a walk-up: a delightful rook's nest. Peggy was pleased to have found a place where it was possible to make loud music without fear of compromising the lease. Stanley, she said, played fast and loud. This apartment remained home to the couple for eighteen months, until Peggy moved to Greenwich Village.

At first Peggy found work in the office of a refugee committee. This was short-lived, and she then took a position in an office organising lease-lend for India. She worked at this second job for a year. Following this, she became a freelancer for a number of American fashion magazines. It seemed she was not to escape an association with clothes, so she decided to cultivate it. She had a strong sense of design and, as she said sarcastically, 'The journalists preferred to talk of clothing'. No doubt Peggy had to take whatever work was offering. She was not a US citizen. She had few skills outside music and freelance writing, neither of which she could expect to find in the short term as an unknown and a foreigner.

Much later in 1947 when Peggy's career was established, the *Sydney Morning Herald* made note of these jobs and quoted her saying that she found the freelance work 'fun' but 'frightfully hectic'. She said:

> 'It involved finding out which movie star was in town, scouting around for some fabulous garment to dress her up in, teeing up jewels, furs and accessories, and then having the whole thing photographed at the fashion exhibition or show of the moment. The worst thing was writing the caption and packing all the information into half an inch.'[9]

Peggy also worked as a freelance arranger for various musical firms and began work on a series of articles on American composers. She sold these to musical publications and glossy magazines. Within eighteen months she confessed in interviews that she had made New York her home, and was planning to take out American citizenship, which she did. It was a strategic move in her career, enabling her to apply for funding from a number of American arts authorities. As an Australian she was ineligible for any musical grants.

When Stanley arrived in New York with Peggy, both were regarded as interesting by popular American composers because of their graduation from the 'Baker's Shop', as Nadia Boulanger's training was called. Only American composers of note had had this privilege. In New York Stanley was already considered an up-and-coming English composer. Recognised as prominent in London's ballet and theatre activities, brochures put out by Associated Music Publishers Inc., New York, described him as 'a moving spirit in theatrical productions during the earlier parts of the war'. He was also said to have toured Australia in the earlier part of 1941 as a lecturer in British and contemporary music, and to have appeared as a soloist in performances of his piano concertos. While these activities are certainly true, the suggestion of an invitation to tour is exaggerated. Clippings from Australian newspapers reveal that these events and appearances occurred randomly when Stanley happened to be available.

Stanley received a Guggenheim Award for composition in New York City in 1942, and during the same year appeared as a soloist in his Concerto for Piano and Orchestra at Carnegie Hall with Sir Thomas Beecham conducting. The following year his work Concertante for Piano and Strings was performed at Carnegie Hall, this time played by the New York Philharmonic Symphony Orchestra under Bruno Walter. A review of this second work entitled 'British Composer to play melody with Philharmonic' appeared in the *New York World Telegram* featuring a picture of Mr and Mrs Stanley Bate. Stanley described Walter's response to the piece. 'I played it for him and he said, "Well it looks mechanical but it sounds romantic".' Romantic was a word that always offended Stanley, but he was grateful for Walter's acceptance and appeared as soloist alongside him on opening night. Stanley had always regarded Walter as a Bach, Beethoven or Brahms 'who bends a skeptical ear to bi-tonal work'.

During this time Stanley also wrote incidental music for Sidney Kingsley's new play *The Patriots*, which opened at the National Theatre the same week as his Carnegie Hall appearance. The play, based on the life of Thomas Jefferson, won the Critics' Award for the best production in 1943. In the previous year Stanley's work Sinfonietta No. 1 was acclaimed at the 1942 International Festival of Contemporary Music. His String Quartet was also premiered by the Lerner Quartet at Town Hall in New York City. His music was described by Alfred Frankenstein in the *New York Times* as 'Fundamentally contemporary in idiom . . . but sure-fire with audiences'.

It had been a momentous year for Stanley, and another invisible one for Peggy. Stanley was becoming cocky about his success and it seemed he had every reason to be. The *New York World Telegram* quoted him as saying 'Perhaps 80 per cent of modern music is of no value. It will be the work of posterity to see what 20 per cent should be saved.'

Peggy cringed at some of his thoughtless press statements. She had again fallen into the role of carer and adviser to Bate. Still she was proud of her husband's success, and prepared to excuse his impossible behaviour as being the guise of a genius. Stanley had a gift for lifting life out of the ordinary and this was one of the qualities that Peggy both admired and worried about. He dressed, drank and entertained lavishly. He loved attending parties and visiting the most eccentric bars he could find in New York, often risking Peggy's physical safety. Increasingly, he spent less time with his wife. It was known that the two separated from each other on social outings anyway. He spent his money as quickly as he earned it and was irresponsible when it came to domestic expenses. Peggy's efforts to keep the bills paid were matched by Stanley's flamboyance.

Peggy was not critical and basked in the success of her husband, believing that her own efforts might soon lead to success. One day she explained her ambitions to Stanley, expecting a sympathetic ear. He had been supported by her, as she saw it, in building his career, and now she wanted some time to compose. She hoped he would offer to pay a few domestic bills while she travelled to research some new music materials. But her old college rival was not to prove a willing ally and two days after this conversation took place he left on a European holiday. He wrote her letters suggesting she give up the apartment and live more cheaply as he planned to be absent intermittently over the coming months. This was the only solution he offered and the matter of her research was considered closed.

Stanley suffered a second breakdown during this successful period after their arrival in New York. The cause of this state of mind remains unknown. He was not emotionally strong and perhaps needed Peggy's strength to sustain him. His second breakdown seems to have contributed to the demise of their relationship. Peggy was a rock of support to him during his success and indeed directly after, but to her friends it seemed she was beginning to tire. She had increasingly established a solid network of friends in New York and spent a great deal of time socialising with them.

The doctor who tended Stanley during the second break-down advised Peggy to get him away from music, believing music to be the main factor to have caused his sudden collapse. Peggy dutifully bought her husband a box of paints and set him to work in a relaxed environment at home. She stayed home with him, drawing an income from articles on music. Initially she thought his paintings pitiful and was disappointed with his efforts, but she encouraged him as best she could, and Stanley's work began to show signs of improvement. She would stare at him when he wasn't looking and described him as being 'locked into a museum of music. There was no person there, just the art. Away from music he appeared just like anyone else, but within music there was no Stanley.'

The improvement in his painting seemed to cheer Stanley up enough to engage in conversation with Peggy again. Inspired by his former teacher Ralph Vaughan Williams' song *In Windsor Forest*, he set to work recreating the image and emotion on canvas. He had visited the exact location with Peggy during their courting days and it gave him a new lease of energy to revisit it through painting. Peggy organised for some of his paintings to appear in minor exhibitions and he was fortunate enough to sell two. This small success got him on his feet, and he returned again to composition. Painting had provided an outlet outside music and for the first time he relaxed. He and Peggy would visit galleries together. She had always been a gallery enthusiast and herself painted with some precision but was too self-critical to exhibit. Two paintings by Bate were hung in Peggy's Paddington house in Sydney, 'Windsor Forest' and an untitled work inspired by the Aboriginal painters that Bate observed during their stay in Australia during the war.

After his return to composition Stanley again drifted away from Peggy. He took trips to London, staying away for months at a time. Peggy began to compose music, and a great number of publications were accepting unsolicited music stories from her. She had used much of her spare time, when not being a wife or breadwinner, pondering the developmental changes music was taking and reading every musical review she could lay her hands on. It seemed there was a market for fresh ideas. Peggy began to write with enthusiasm and miraculously, as it seemed to her, her work began to appear in small magazines.

Peggy had achieved nothing musically in Australia and was aware that she would have to make opportunities for herself in New York. Stanley was obviously never going to play fair. That is, he was never going to put his career on temporary hold and help out with the domestic bills. Peggy had faced frequent phone disconnections, an occasional summons, not to mention the humiliation of borrowing money from friends. She had made it possible for him to explore his work and could not believe his refusal to assist her. It was clear to her that she would always have to be both composer and provider. They were not 'working to help each other' as they had previously agreed, but as Stanley's absences grew more frequent her own financial position showed signs of improvement. Given her more satisfactory state of mind, her composition began to increase both in quantity and quality.

An interview by journalist Elizabeth Auld from the *Herald*'s

London bureau captured some of this new energy. It tells that Mrs P. Bate has been working on peculiar instrumental combinations, as well as experimental work for percussion and speech choruses; and that she has plans to compose a dance cantata with a speaking ballet. Her critical knowledge of music was recorded: 'P. Bates,' says the journalist, 'is writing for the New York *Music Courier* and several other music publications. She has been asked by the Grove's *Dictionary of Music* publishers to research several American composers for inclusion in their next edition.'

Peggy described her household to one journalist as 'separated by a piano'. She explained there was only one piano in the home, the other in storage or elsewhere depending on her husband's work abroad. Peggy rarely played when Stanley was home. 'He plays only all day and half the night!' said Peggy. She made distinctions between Stanley's work and her own. 'Stanley works on a big massive scale, my work is highly specialised, dealing mostly with less usual instrumental groups.'

As usual this article gave the factual content of Peggy's work, but this time Peggy was provocative about her personal life rather than about music. She anticipated the journalist's outrage about her husband's selfishness. That she expected it indicates something of her changing attitude. There is also a hint of growing confidence in this interview. This time she would prove unstoppable.

NOTES

1. Douglas Gilbert, *New York World Telegram*, 28 Jan. 1943.
2. Peggy Glanville-Hicks, in interview with author, 1987.
3. The Melbourne *Age*, 23 Nov. 1940.
4. *ABC Weekly*, 1940.
5. *Sydney Morning Herald*, 'Women's Supplement', 29 Oct. 1940.
6. 1940 article, undated, no byline, P. G.-H. clippings book (Red), State Library of Victoria.
7. Melbourne *Age*, 23 Nov. 1940.
8. The *Herald*, 9 June 1940.
9. The *Australian Herald*, 1947.

Myrtle Glanville-Hicks, Peggy's mother.

Ernest Glanville-Hicks, Peggy's father.

Beric Glanville-Hicks, Peggy's brother.

Peggy — a composer in the making.

Esther Rofe and Peggy.

Stanley Bate, Peggy's husband.

above
Stanley Bate,
Peggy's husband.

right
Nadia Boulanger

Peggy

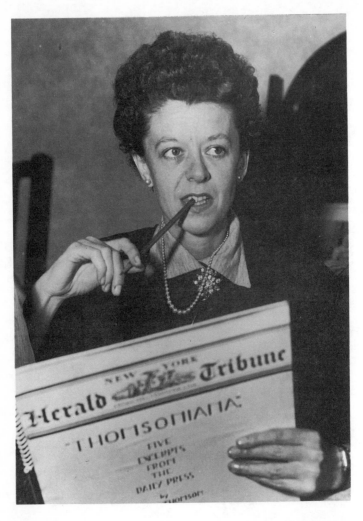

Peggy when she worked at the *New York Herald-Tribune*.

Virgil Thompson, Peggy's boss at the
New York Herald-Tribune.

Peggy at work with author Robert Graves in Greece.

Peggy and Paul Bowles in New York.

Peggy at the opening performance of *Nausicaa*
in Greece. On her left is choreographer John Butler,
on her right is Robert Graves.

Peggy at an international composers' forum.

Peggy in New York.

COMPOSER FOR THEATRE

P. GLANVILLE - HICKS

FOUR OPERAS

FIVE BALLETS

left
Composer
for Theatre
program.

below
Peggy
working on
Sappho with
Lawrence
Durrell.

Peggy at home in Paddington with the
painted fresco behind her.

Roger Glanville-Hicks, Peggy's nephew.

left
Portrait of
Peggy by
Joyce
McGrath.

below
Peggy
receiving her
honorary
doctorate at
the University
of Sydney
with
Australian
composer
Peter
Sculthorpe.

Peggy with Wendy Beckett.

THE *NEW YORK*
HERALD - TRIBUNE
(1 9 4 0 – 5 0)

When Peggy first decided to have her biography written, she believed research would begin and end with her time in New York. In retrospect, this was how she saw her life. As her biographer I wanted to meet everyone she had known to piece together the missing parts of her life. After two years research, including a three and a half month world tour retracing her steps, I uncovered many details. It was obvious that her story did not cease in New York. Life cannot be so compartmentalised.

I visited the Royal College of Music in London and spoke with some of her old college friends: Joseph Horovitz, Sir Lennox Berkeley, John Gardner, Dr Geoffrey Bush. I even stumbled across an old lover of Stanley Bate's who described him for me: 'He was immaculately dressed always, pleasant, likeable, sculptured, quietly handsome like a bank manager. He wrote his best work in the early fifties, the piano sonata. A soon vanished *good* composer. I met him forty years ago. Ah, to hear his name uttered aloud, it lives again.' This composer preferred not to be named. Dr Geoffrey Bush, another colleague of Stanley's, described his first symphony which was performed alongside Stanley Bate's work: 'He got better reviews than I did. I was struck by the inventiveness of his music, especially his third symphony.'

None of these people could comment on his marriage to Peggy. However, one interview did turn up a red herring concerning Peggy's marriages—plural. I was too astonished and the person with the knowledge clammed up. He rephrased his statement—'I think she married a young musician who was living with me in California.' I was unable to find any records. At a later stage in my research two of her friends from New York, Oliver Daniels and Jac Murphy, thought there had been a marriage of convenience to an Israeli man who needed citizenship for a green card. It may have been true but I was not granted access to the records.

I pondered the lack of attention to detail these friends of hers paid. Did she trivialise her love life in humour? Was it just fanciful ideas that she spoke of to friends? Would this explain their lack of knowledge? Whatever the truth about the facts of her life, she did not want them all discovered. She was adamant that only one history of her married life be told. Stanley Bate was her husband and she loved him because of his talent and beauty. The other story was that Paul Bowles, the American novelist, was the true love of her life whose talent, eccentricity, intellect and humour went unmatched. Rather than revealing all to a female biographer as she had promised me, she was editing her life story.

I continued my journey: Tangiers, Morocco, Greece, New York. She had been correct in her dramatic assessment of her place in the New York world. Even the secretaries of those I visited were in awe of the once well-known P.G.-H. A comment or two would float across a phone conversation or waiting room, 'I met her once.'

New York, it seemed, was the centre of the universe. Peggy wrote indefatigably on modern composers and modern music and began to carve out a name for herself as a reliable music critic. Then in 1947, after years of piecemeal work, she was offered a job as music critic on the *New York Herald-Tribune*. She was also finally becoming the composer she had imagined herself to be. Despite the slow start in composition while married to Stanley Bate, she had a modest list of works behind her that she had completed as a student, as well as work she had produced for the 1938 International Society of Contemporary Music Festival. These included an opera, three ballets, concerti for flute and for piano, a sinfonia, a cantata and numerous chamber pieces. She arranged for two or three of these to be printed. However, her reputation as a composer was not to begin until 1945 when her Concertino da Camera was recorded by Columbia. This gave her a small audience.

An article written in 1950 by Peggy's employer Virgil Thomson, chief music critic of the *New York Herald-Tribune*, encapsulates the world of music that Peggy was a part of. His article traced the beginnings of modernism. 'France,' he wrote, 'had given the world Debussy and Ravel.' He described their impressionistic techniques. 'Austria had produced Schoenberg and his school, and with him came the expressionist aesthetics, the use of atonal harmony as a psychological microscope.' In Russia he cited the emergence of successes such as Igor Stravinsky and in ballet, Sergey Diaghilev. He also examined the effects on music of the Second World War and its relation to modernism. 'Neo-classicism,' he claimed, 'was the official aesthetic everywhere; a romantic invention, tainted for the modernists by its associations with Mendelssohn and Brahms and rediscovered by Debussy and the impressionists.' Modernism still eluded almost everyone.

Peggy was impressed with Thomson. She saw the potential for expanding her own view in future articles under Thomson's editorship. She had begun to agree with Thomson, despite her contrary views on neo-classicism. Atonalism had started to rise again while the neo-classicists were on the wane. Atonal schools were first popular in the late twenties when Alban Berg's opera *Wozzeck* became a hit in Central Europe. It felt strangely reminiscent. The smoke of the Second World War had blown away and it seemed a musical liberation had taken place. The world's musical centre was no longer Europe, it was America—to the Americans at least; and the emergence of an American school of composition was finally a reality. New York was regarded as the musical stock exchange, the centre of stabilisation for musical opinion, or so it seemed between 1940 and 1950.[1]

During Peggy's second week of employment at the *New York Herald-Tribune*, Thomson's sequel to the 1940–1950 article was published. In this piece he singled out the three countries he regarded as capable of producing good quality music: France, Russia and the United States. By this he meant publicly pleasing yet serious music. He neglected to mention Benjamin Britten or any of the other English composers who were enjoying international success. Next Thomson turned to film in America: 'During the 1950s film contributed little to music and if anything added expense.' He was optimistic about radio but said that it tended to 'distribute rather than create music.'[2] Whenever Thomson wrote he was well received. Regarded as a central force, newcomers to New York gravitated towards him, Peggy among them. She and Stanley Bate had identified themselves with Thomson's definition of contemporary music. His articles met with their support.

Virgil and his colleagues comprised the music circle musicians and composers longed to be part of. It was during the early to mid-forties that Virgil first appointed Peggy to the *New York Herald-Tribune* as music critic, having noticed her reviews in other publications. While the financial rewards were not enormous Peggy was none the less flattered. At the *New York Herald-Tribune* Peggy joined six other music critics, covering the vast array of concerts being given across the USA, particularly in New York. Music performances had increased in number since the end of the war.

At home Australia was making musical history. The Sydney Symphony Orchestra was forming out of the ABC with subsidies from the State Government and the City Council. The ABC had also set up orchestras in all six states. The Arts Council of Australia had formed and a Commonwealth Film Unit was newly established.

Elsewhere, Maria Callas was making her debut in Ponchielli's *La Gioconda* at Verona. (At this stage she and Peggy had not met.) Gian Carlo Menotti opened in New York with two new operas *The Medium* and *The Telephone*. Carlo and Peggy had met briefly and were later to become close friends. Pablo Casals publicly vowed during this time never to play in Spain while Franco was in power. Benjamin Britten was at his best, producing the opera *Albert Herring* at Glyndebourne. Tennessee Williams had just won the Pulitzer prize for drama for his play *A Streetcar Named Desire*. New York was enjoying a perpetual arts and musical festival and the *New York Herald-Tribune* was recording every moment.

Owned by Ogden Reid, the *New York Herald-Tribune* leaned editorially in the direction of liberal republicanism. Its readership consisted of the cultured and intellectual. Its circulation was 450,000 in 1947–48 and continued to grow, the weekly book section extending to 750,000 during Peggy's time. While not a massive output by today's standards, much of its appeal lay in the columnists of the day, Virgil Thomson being the obvious favourite. Under his editorship the world musical scene was well reported for fourteen sparkling seasons.

The *New York Herald-Tribune* was laid out in a similar fashion to the *New York Times*. The inside page gave a list of the events covered. World politics featured in the first column daily and other subjects included Washington events, city and vicinity of New York, sports, financial markets, editorials and miscellany and, of course, music. In the year Peggy joined the newspaper, the front pages ranged from the partitioning of India into India and Pakistan, followed by Gandhi's assassination, and the election of Harry S. Truman as President of the United States.

In sharp contrast to these world changes, the music section continued with leading stories by Virgil Thomson expounding on the importance of understanding modern music. Thomson's targets included those who decried exaggerated musical change, citing the work of offenders such as Strauss, Debussy, Ravel, Schoenberg, Stravinsky and Satie. He enjoyed harking back to the revolutionary years, the 'other' war as he called it. His audience relied on his acerbic wit and information to impress at parties. Some read for his ideas.

Virgil liked to give a quick educative précis of the various schools of musical thought to reassure the reader that modern music was entirely accessible. His clever use of language and relaxed journalistic style did much to demystify and explain the ever-changing focus of music during the forties and fifties.

He explained to the reader that 'dead music; that whole baroque, rococo and romantic repertory we call "classical" is as comfortable and as solacing to mental inactivity as a lullaby heard on a pillow made from the down of a defunct swan'.

He would include subheadings on modern music which read, 'New Music costs money, but it is the life of the party'. Never one to miss an opportunity, he would sometimes take a stand and make recommendations about modern music at the end of a story such as, 'Modern Music requires continuous opportunity for its practise at Carnegie Hall. This is the only means for restoring our major orchestras to their rightful place in our intellectual life.'[3]

In New York it was possible for critics and composers alike to find a platform on which to discuss ideas and the direction of music as well as creating the humble review.

Peggy's first weeks on the job passed without incident. She wrote an innocuous review containing just a smattering of her musical discoveries. Her early reviews were tiny in length and tucked away behind more newsworthy arts details. In particular, there was gossip about Greta Garbo, the death of the opera singer Mary Lewis, the first official display of women's civilian defence uniforms, the opening of plays-of-the-week such as *Papa Is All* by Patterson Green at the Guild Theatre, and *The Lady Comes Across* by Fred Thompson. The Duchess of Windsor's favourite recipes were even included. Each edition featured musical review and entertainment pages with extensive commentary.

Peggy's office at the *Tribune* was a tiny little compartment behind a partition. In each of these mini-rooms was a wooden desk. Manual typewriters clicked away like bees. Peggy worked in complete isolation, always writing by hand first, followed by a quick type-up, before initialling the piece P.G.-H. These initials became the affectionate pen name by which she was known to readers.

Peggy would aim to include in each first paragraph an account of who was doing what and where. In the second paragraph she would offer a word or two on the program. In the third paragraph she would move onto critical explanation of the piece. She tried with considerable effort to write 'uncuttable sentences', assuming what she termed her P.G.-H. theory—that a tight structure would prevent editing. Because of her position she gained free tickets to almost every musical concert or production in New York. These included shows she was not even scheduled to review. Aside from the reviews, this bonus made an otherwise financially meagre life stimulating.

As she grew confident her reviews grew in length. They often ran to four columns. She did not relinquish her work for other musical magazines either, such as the *Juilliard Review* and *The American Composers' Alliance*. In these publications she could take her views further, giving lengthy commentary. Indirectly this added credence to her *Tribune* reviews. In *The American Composers' Alliance*, for example, a four-page story–review of Arthur Berger appeared.

> The big leaps in the melodic lines are perhaps the most arresting feature in all Berger's work; the style today is diatonic—though it was not always so, but the leaps and intensive fragmentation of the melodic parts are more related to the twelve tone composers, Berg, and even more so to Webern, than to the neo-classicists of whom Berger is considered one. These leaps, on a diatonic rather than an atonal or row basis, are really a continuous process of passing note or appoggiatura note to the implied or stated harmonic progression.[4]

These detailed musical analyses were much respected in the musical world. For the general public she was less academic, although she could never resist opinion. A memorial article about Olin Downes (1886–1955) written by Peggy during the early fifties offers a hint of her writing style.

> Olin Downes had a kind of radar for musicality, for the intangible but powerful impulse that is at the heart of all

real music . . . In an age of specialised personalities, this grand humanitarian, like a man strayed from the Renaissance, was a leaven in our over-clever world, and we will miss him sadly.[5]

Peggy's bold responses became almost as notable as her reviews. She always accorded the reader the respect due to intellect. She was combative but rarely condescending. She penned the following letter to an editor defending herself against an argumentative reader. Unfortunately, the letter the reader sent is lost, but her retort gives an indication of her style as music critic as well as explaining something of her practice as a composer.

Dear Sir,

I would like to thank Mr El-Dabh for his lively comments on my article of Feb 9th—an article whose precise meaning was alas somewhat impaired by the need for simplification, and by the unavoidable space cuts that included the cutting of its original title, 'Westward to the East'.

I believe Mr El-Dabh's view and mine closely coincide except in definition of terms; in Western usage there is no such concept as that of melodic dissonance, the word dissonance implying to us vertical combination of simultaneously heard sounds of tense, stringent nature—or similar vertical implication at a given moment of moving parts.

It is a curious fact that Eastern melodic composition, couched as it is in terms of modal 'row' or raga gives an impression of harmony, the tones heard in sequence remaining cumulatively in the ear as an effect of combination.

By the same token, when the Eastern melody is embellished with the rich variety of arabesques, appoggiaturas or 'bent' time decorations that embody not only dissonant intervals, but also quarter and lesser fractional intervals, the effect is certainly one of dissonance, and it is actually melodically achieved.

The oriental use of dissonance to which Mr El-Dabh refers is so much a part of the instruments on which it is played, and even more, of the personal improvisatory virtuosity factor of the performer–creator of Eastern tradition that any attempt to transfer these effects to Western instrumentation is not only not possible, but I think, invalid.

My opposition is not to dissonance as such, but only to the seemingly compulsive and indiscriminate use (especially by the younger composers, and at the expense of mastery of more basic factors) as though it were the sole and automatic badge of 'modernity'.

What I am advocating is an investigation into the science embodied in the tone relationships of the basic ragas of the Hindus, and into their complex metrical system and its relevance to melodic structure.

These, being based—as are our own fundamentals—on the overtone series and on mathematical permutation, are essentially available to us within our own instrumental gamut without infringement save that implicit in the tempered scale, which in itself is a slight infringement of pure acoustical law.[6]

Peggy Glanville-Hicks

It is likely that when Peggy first settled in New York she perceived her social connections as work, and made efforts to be liked. Like all role-playing this was not to last. Her Australian accent tinged with the influence of Kensington was probably as much a product of her private school in Victoria as of her five years at the Royal College of Music and marriage to an English husband. In any case she never altered her speech to win acceptance, and despite many years in New York she never acquired an American accent. This peculiar voice distinguished her in Greenwich Village. There she was recognised for her strong will and, as author Paul Bowles once put it: 'She may have a soft voice but is definitely a woman to be reckoned with in intellectual debate.'

Of all her colleagues and acquaintances during her days on the *Tribune* none were more special than Paul Bowles, then a practising composer. Peggy especially liked to tell how she and Paul Bowles met. She had been fed a gossipy story that Bowles, music critic on the *New York Herald-Tribune*, had gone stone deaf. The reason for this, she was told, was because he wanted to be a novelist, not a composer. The illness was said to be entirely psychosomatic. Rumour had it that his hearing had improved the moment he resigned as a music critic. Peggy was more interested in the vacancy he had left at the *Tribune* than in his disabilities, but none the less continued to circulate this good story.

Shortly after her initiation into the social circles of the *New York Herald-Tribune* she attended a party being given by a Mrs Murray Cran. It was the usual music gathering and she was chatting to Aaron Copland, who no doubt added his own pieces to the story of Paul's deafness, for he had been Paul's teacher as well as friend. When Paul arrived at the party he was immediately noticed by Peggy. 'He was standing in the middle of the room,' she said, 'holding a drink, this golden-haired fabulous creature, and without taking my eyes from him I clutched Aaron's arms and said impulsively, "Introduce me".'

Peggy, hearing the name Paul Bowles, raised the pitch of her voice. It was some way into the conversation before Paul's awkward stares alerted her to drop the volume. Paul had perfect hearing. He explained that the story had been exaggerated. Peggy was acutely embarrassed. Paul was laughing. The attention the two lavished on each other at the party led certain guests at the party to mistake Paul for Stanley or Peggy for Jane Bowles. This delighted Peggy who proudly exclaimed that she and Paul were twins. Her reasoning was based on the coincidence of their birthdays, although Paul was in fact born on the next day New York time and was one year older. She omitted this detail from her story.

In Tangiers, in 1989, in an apartment furnished with heavy hessian curtains and chestnut-coloured cushions, I sat down with Paul Bowles to discuss Peggy. This was the man whom Peggy had described as forever thirty years of age, with honey blond hair and finely chiselled good looks. Paul recalled for me their first meeting.

I think I met Peg in Central Park where a concert was being given. She was with her husband Stanley Bate. I was with Jane [Bowles]. Peggy loved to talk about music and so of course there was an immediate attraction between us. Jane was bored by talk of music, or perhaps Peg bored her. Anyway the four of us changed positions on the street. I walked with Peg, and well, I suppose Jane and Stanley walked together— or perhaps alone, I don't remember. Peg and I were getting on famously. Stanley stopped us all at one point, announcing, 'You should have married Paul Bowles instead of me.' If it was jealousy that had gripped him, it didn't affect anyone and nothing else was said on the way to the concert arena.

From this evening on, Paul and Peggy became constant companions. Paul would visit Peggy whenever Stanley was out. They would phone first and arrange to meet, usually at Peggy's apartment. Paul told in his autobiography, *Without Stopping*, of an ugly incident when he called by unexpectedly without phoning. Much to his surprise he noticed a trail of blood outside Peggy's apartment. It led curiously in the direction of her front door. When he opened the door he discovered that the source of the blood trail led to Peggy herself.

'But, what's happened?' exclaimed Paul.

'It's Stanley,' said Peggy. 'Didn't you know? He beats me.'

Bowles was enraged. In his autobiography he depicts Bate as a violent drunkard. One would suspect Paul of jealousy, except that other details reveal that Bate did have a drinking problem. Peggy did not write to Paul about the disclosures he had made, but her embarrassment and disapproval were known to friends.

Paul and Peggy's friendship began as one of mutual intrigue because of their similar background in composition and criticism. Peggy was a great admirer of Paul's music, and even went so far as to spend time making musical calligraphy copies of his unpublished scores, no doubt to ensure his survival in history.

From Virgil Thomson to John Cage the gossip mounted, and it soon became public knowledge that there was more than music involved in this special friendship. Peggy had fallen in love with Paul. Peggy continued to describe her relationship with Paul as one of 'twinship'. In reality it had grown to be much more; the two were inseparable and after several months they became lovers. Much was made of their common birthday. When people described the two as looking alike, they were referring to dress style. Peggy preferred to wear slacks and jackets or skirts with a gentleman's tie.

According to Peggy, Jane Bowles was a lesbian and Stanley homosexual. Fate had intervened and brought her and Paul together, Peggy said, yet she sometimes described her lover as bisexual. Doubt also fell on her own sexual preference. She was seen as a woman surrounded by homosexual men. It is difficult to separate the facts from the truth, but Peggy felt drawn to Paul as if by fate. Jane Bowles' presence did not appear to be a problem.

In Tangiers Paul told me the story of how he and Jane first met. Towards the end of the thirties some of his friends had been talking about the writer Jane Auer. Described as something of a free spirit, Paul was anxious to meet this woman. One night walking along Broadway, he spied two beautiful young women hanging out of the door of a black automobile, laughing and haranguing the driver. He recognised one of the women as Erika Mann, daughter of Thomas Mann, and to his surprise she introduced him to her red-haired friend Jane Auer. The two women were on their way to Harlem to smoke marijuana and Paul was invited along for the ride. He accepted. Paul was captivated by the charm and wit of Jane Auer. 'She was quite wonderful. I've never met anyone like her, in the *least* like her. Full of so many ideas, never a bore, always something new.'

They dated frequently and were married within a year in 1938. Paul persuaded Jane to join him in Tangiers and she too fell in love with Morocco. Perhaps because of the influence of his writer wife, or perhaps out of a desire to extend beyond surrealist poetry, Paul turned to fiction.

It was during a visit to New York that he first met Peggy, who was to replace him as music critic on the *New York Herald-Tribune*. When she first took the job she initialled the column P.B. (Peggy Bate, a name she had never used before), and seemed to enjoy the confusion of being regarded as Paul Bowles, and indistinguishable by their initials. Paul knew nothing of this ambiguity, but Peggy prided herself in being able to take over the column without her readers detecting the change of critic. In a short time the novelty wore off and she began to initial the column by her pen name P.G.-H.

Paul's background alone fascinated Peggy, and if she had a weakness for men of any type, it was for men with musical genius. She and Paul shared a mutual friend in composer Aaron Copland. Before Peggy's arrival in New York, Copland had travelled with Paul to Tangiers, where the two men had settled down to work in a cottage high in the mountains of Morocco. Paul took lessons every day. Copland had organised a schedule to ensure time for his own work as well as completing the task of educating Paul. Paul was a patient student and amused himself writing surrealist poetry during the times that Aaron was busy composing. As the months passed, Copland became agitated with the isolation and left for Berlin. Paul had grown attached to Tangiers and decided to stay on. He surveyed the property market and made plans to return permanently. But his plans remained only plans, and by the end of the year he was forced to return to New York for financial reasons.

In New York he set up house with poet W. H. Auden and composer Benjamin Britten. Other residents in this same house at Brooklyn Heights had been Gypsy Rose Lee, George Davis, Thomas Mann's son Golo, British tenor Peter Pears, and Oliver Smith. A regular visitor to the house was Salvador Dali, whose work George Davis had brought home from the office of *Harper's Bazaar*, where he was editor. Paul recalled an incident in which some of Dali's sketches were accidentally left on a window ledge and spoiled by the rain.

Paul began working as a music critic on the *New York Herald-Tribune*. He befriended a new visitor to the house, a young playwright called Tennessee Williams. Williams was looking for someone to compose music for his plays. Paul was delighted at the prospect of composing for the theatre and wrote scores for four of Williams' plays: *The Glass Menagerie, Summer and Smoke, Sweet Bird of Youth* and *The Milk Train Doesn't Stop Here Anymore*. As a composer he also had had to his credit *Watcher on the Rhine* by Lillian Hellman, and *Liberty Jones* by Phillip Barry, both of which won critics' praise across the country.

In 1949 Paul's literary career began to develop when his first novel, *The Sheltering Sky*, was published and received high acclaim. An addiction to writing overtook him and music began to take second place. Three more novels were to follow in quick succession: *Let It Come Down, The Spiders' House* and *Up Above The World*, confirming for him a secure reputation. His work had found an audience.

I discovered much about Bowles that was at odds with the person I was speaking to. From reading his works I came to understand an author who relished taboos—incest, hedonism and perversity. A sense of anxiety and dread pervades his work. Dominant themes include: the elemental clash between the primitive and the civilised; and the psychic disintegration and moral decay which overtakes characters confronting the primitive. He was preoccupied by contrasts, themes of naivety and guile, puritan restraint and pagan indulgence, western sophistication and ancient superstition. And he dished the whole lot up all at once, confronting readers directly, demanding that they seek out the horrors that lie below the cultural fabric. To Paul Bowles, all cultures are alien and the shelter 'we hide and grovel beneath' is without walls to protect us. Some of his short stories are considered quite shocking; penises are cut off, adolescent boys seduce their fathers, corpses are desecrated—anything could happen and often does. When I asked him to explain this, he said, almost purring: 'I love stories that begin very amusingly and end in the most ghastly tragedy.' Bowles liked to arouse panic and insecurity in the reader.

At the time of knowing Peggy, Tangiers had allowed him to combine a lifestyle and a writing career that he found congenial (as indeed he still does). Peggy's relationship with Bowles continued throughout the forties and fifties by letter. Meanwhile, Peggy's life in New York was blossoming and neither she nor Paul considered leaving their spouses. Stanley remained an obsession for Peggy, just as Jane did for Paul. The Bowles had an unusual understanding between them, and while Jane always lived separately from Paul this did not weaken their bond. Both felt a freedom to pursue career and relationship as it took them, at least in theory. According to Peggy, Jane usually rented apartments adjacent to Paul's.

In New York at the time Peggy and Paul were together, Jane was living in a stormy relationship with a woman several years older than herself. Jane's involvement with Paul proved the stronger bond, for when Paul moved back to his haven in Tangiers, Jane chose to go with him. However, Jane became restless at times, making many more trips back to New York than Paul. In Tangiers she anchored herself in the flat below Paul's. During visits to Europe and the United States she would collect material for her short stories and organise publication of her work. Paul was an ally in her work life, and assisted her in editing and selecting stories for publication. In the early 1970s, after many years of being nursed by Paul and after several breakdowns, a series of strokes finally killed her. If Paul's loyalty to Jane seemed unbreakable, so was his bond to Peggy.

Peggy adored the bizarre behaviour of Bowles. He seemed flamboyant, polished; he spoke four languages: French, English, Arabic and Spanish. Everything about him was exciting. After Paul's long stay in Tangiers during the fifties Peggy saw much less of him, although she visited Tangiers, and thousands of letters spanning a lifetime passed between them. Bowles' life as a writer continued to flourish and he kept Peggy posted on his successes, including his translation of Jean-Paul Sartre's play *No Exit*. Sartre apparently read the work aloud in French to a youthful Bowles in a Greenwich Village cafe, and Bowles translated at the table directly into English, finishing in just one and a half hours. This translation remains current.

Virgil Thomson agreed to be interviewed at his Chelsea Hotel apartment in July 1989, just three months before his death at ninety-three. Memories of the *New York Herald-Tribune* days brought a faint smile to an otherwise steely gaze. He was almost completely deaf. He asked me to stand three feet back from him and shout the questions. An impatient retired editor and composer, he was not an easy interviewee. After rephrasing a question for himself, he would offer the necessary response.

'We were all there—Harrison, Perkins, Robert Lawrence, Jerome Bohn, Paul Bowles—a great staff. Everyone socialised and worked together. During the war we ran short of help [with reviewing musical productions] and took on stringers such as Peggy Glanville-Hicks. At one stage we had eight altogether reviewing music. Our aim was to review everything that took place.' He described the task of reviewing. 'A reviewing position is ideal for a composer. It takes just the time of the concert, plus one hour. One's identity is what one does in the daytime. Reviews are only to earn money. One is not both a reviewer and a composer. One is only a composer.'

Thomson said that Peggy was employed because she was 'one of us'. By this he meant that she had passed through the Bakery. Peggy was the only female music critic on the *Tribune*. The few other women employed by the paper worked in secretarial areas. Peggy had a sense of being alone. In later life she celebrated this as a victory. At the time, given her practical approach to life, she wanted her gender to go unnoticed. There were no women critics before her and so she was her own guide, approaching the task as an academic male might. She gained no special favours by her gender and abhorred such notions. She maintained the view that 'quality is the only criterion'. She believed that her level of expertise would obliterate any form of discrimination. As a stringer she was paid on space rates according to what she did. 'I didn't put up with fools,' Virgil Thomson said. 'They [the critics] had to know their business and review curiously and correctly.'

Thomson described the context in which he placed Peggy musically: 'Peggy, like many composers who graduated from the Royal College of Music, had been strongly influenced by Ralph Vaughan Williams, unlike the Schoenberg pupils. Nadia Boulanger's teachings formed the commonground link between P.G.-H.'s musical views and the rest of the US composers.' Thomson paused to think, 'She was of Australian opinion,' he said. 'She became a US citizen but it didn't alter her character!'

His first recollection of meeting Peggy was at a function with her husband Stanley Bate. Thomson recalled that they 'didn't get on too well' but he also remembered a meeting with Peggy and his other stringer Paul Bowles. 'Well,' Thomson said, 'everyone liked Paul; he was an accomplished writer, useful. And everyone liked Peggy; she had talent and perception and, well, they were madly in love. It was obvious.'

Thomson, a journalist himself, pre-empted a question on gender. 'Australian women are so bossy.' He expected a response but continued to talk anyway. 'P.G.-H. was the first one [Australian woman] I encountered. We used to have shouting matches. Can you imagine? *I* was her boss man on the *Tribune*!' He paused. 'Peggy was a professional. Why else would I have hired a woman? All my critics were gifted composers. She was a lady composer but she was "one of us". I had to fire her once. She made some foolish joke in a review. You get fired for telling lies, I warned her.'

Peggy's version of this story was that she was sent off to

review an eccentric composer who was performing around New York with a strange percussion instrument that looked and sounded absurd. Other critics had already had the misfortune of covering this particular artist's work, and so Peggy set off wondering what more she could possibly add. Her piece the next day was a little mocking, ending with the statement that 'even the artist's hair was wired for sound'. This seemingly innocuous statement irritated Thomson. That very next morning he walked into Peggy's office and announced: 'Honeychild, I'm gunna have to fire you.' Peggy was surprised but felt confident that her readership would rally to her support. Quietly she went home for a week to put her feet up. By the Friday Thomson had to deal with complaints from the P.G.-H. readers by both mail and telephone. Everyone, apparently, enjoyed the P.G.-H. humour. Thomson reinstated her without a word of apology and never mentioned the incident again.

Pre-empting yet another question, Thomson offered an explanation for Peggy's success: 'I attributed Peggy's success to the fact that she was a talented composer, well-connected through her teachers, and she was Australian and pushy. I hear they have at last heard about her in Australia. It's time!' He glared at me.

Peggy described Thomson behind his back as 'a perfect egg', a 'humpty dumpty', but in fact she had a great deal of admiration for the man who had become the cornerstone of American music. She was especially pleased by his genuine interest and support of contemporary composers. She also respected his music. During 1949 she wrote a ten-page article on Virgil Thomson for the *Musical Quarterly*.[6] She described him as 'one of the most controversial composer figures on the American scene'. She supported her glowing appreciation of his musical technique with an analysis that isolated form and theme, citing actual music script to consolidate her argument. A well researched and documented review, this, like many of her articles, established her as an intellectual of music.[7]

Thomson passed the large story off lightly, but no composer could have resisted such a flattering in-depth breakdown of their own work. A confirmed homosexual, Thomson once said of Peggy Glanville-Hicks: 'If Peggy were a man I would have married her!'

Peggy's position on the *New York Herald-Tribune* had caused some alterations in her life. Stanley came and went, travelling backwards and forwards between London and New York. Each trip to London unsettled Peggy's financial stability though it provided some continuity in their relationship. Wages for review work were not particularly lucrative, and she supplemented them by writing for other publications such as *Vogue* and *Harper's Bazaar*; all the while overcommitting herself to a host of musical organisations where she worked voluntarily, organising concerts and functions. She also did much to advance the work of fellow composers, a lifelong preoccupation.

After one of Stanley's departures, Peggy moved from the upper end of Manhattan down into the Village. Her income had not significantly improved but she found she could afford a smallish bed-sit arrangement nearer her friends, including Virgil Thomson, who always resided at the Chelsea Hotel; Aaron Copland, who was active on almost as many committees as Peggy; Leonard Bernstein, who was just a baby in the musical world at the time, but impressive in his knowledge of musicology; and numerous others who, through music or art, came to occupy a space in her life.

Shortly after Peggy settled into Greenwich Village, the local artistic community, which included: Martha Graham, the choreographer; Gore Vidal, the young novelist; Anaïs Nin the writer and her film-maker, banker husband Ian Hugo; Tennessee Williams, the playwright and his occasional flat-mate Paul Bowles; invited Peggy to join them on a local council committee. Conflicts ranged from the saving of Carnegie Hall to the passing of a bill which would prohibit developers from erecting high-rise buildings any taller than existing structures. The aim was to keep Greenwich Village from becoming walled in on all sides by towering buildings. These and other issues united the artists living there.

Neighbour Anaïs Nin wrote a brief portrait of Peggy Glanville-Hicks at this time, which was later published in her diary:

> She is small, very slender, very quick, with eloquent hands designing patterns in space to illustrate her talk. She has a small, impish face, with innocent sharp focused eyes, a humorous uptilted nose, a dimpled smile. She is decisive, sharp-witted. She wears her hair short like an adolescent, brushed upward. She is a witty polemicist. It does not appear at first like a battle. Her swordplay is invisible, it is done with a smile, but the accuracy of it is deadly. She mocks the composers and the critics who interfere with the development of a woman composer. It was the first time I had heard a brilliant, effective woman demonstrate the obstacles which impaired her professional achievement because she was a woman. I gave her all my books![8]

Anaïs Nin, whose father was a musician and whose brother Joaquín Nin-Culmell was a composer, had a special interest in music and often mirrored the essence of musical structure in her writing style. Naturally she was drawn to Peggy. Anaïs once nursed Peggy through a difficult illness in New York during one of Stanley Bate's exhausting visits. From time to time he would arrive on Peggy's doorstep in need of comfort or money. Usually an argument would ensue. Stanley would have been drinking. He would want to rehash the reasons why their relationship was impossible even though he hadn't the slightest intention of renewing it with her.

Nin was a patient listener and a caring friend during these times. She lived in the next street and she and Peggy had friends in common, such as the violist Walter Trampler. Both shared an incompatibility with Jane Bowles. Anaïs had kindly sent Jane all her books and Jane had failed to respond. Peggy and Ian Hugo (Anaïs Nin's New York husband) would sometimes meet for coffee in the Village during Anaïs' legendary trips to Los Angeles where she visited her other husband, the handsome actor–forester Rupert Pole. Peggy became attracted to Hugo over time but Hugo's interest in women, according to Peggy, was purely platonic.

Other Village friends reliable for coffee and discussion were Leonard Bernstein and Aaron Copland, both of whom would meet with Peggy and discuss the categories of contemporary music and its future. Aaron, like Peggy, was actively involved in music forums and the organising of concerts. Peggy was personally involved in the musical careers of her colleagues and friends and was known to write music for musician friends who were in need of a boost or opportunity in their careers. 'Let's write a world premier,' she would tease, and then do it.

Peggy's compositions were rarely included in the early concert programs in New York, but when she became a leading organiser the question of her inclusion was revised. All of her contemporary male colleagues were eager to be involved in anything new that was happening. As organiser, Peggy made sure her own work featured. She would also include as many other composers as befitted the program. She never nursed any resentment for having been excluded; always a person to change and adjust to her circumstances, she found action a better course than bitchiness, and despised gossip. Peggy became very much a person who could make things happen. Her energy was tireless and her enthusiasm extreme. She enjoyed nearly everything about being a composer and living in New York. Everything, that is, except the high rents.

Apart from Peggy's Village friends, most of whom were artists of some distinction, there was also a coterie of composers and musician friends that met regularly. These people occupied a different sphere in Peggy's life. One such friend was Walter Trampler, for whom she was later to write a viola concerto; one of her many 'world premier pieces'.

In New York in 1989 I spoke with the handsome violist. A charming man with roguish eyes and an infectious laugh, he told a story which ultimately led back to his association with Peggy. He had just arrived back in New York, having been drafted into the forces until 1946. He had the option of performing with the Boston Symphony and making a comfortable living or going to New York to discover what everyone was referring to as 'modern music'. Trampler believed it was necessary to 'be there at the right time with the goods' and for him this meant New York. He, like many other composers and musicians arriving back in town, was trying to pick up what remained of a once vital career. He teamed up with some others and formed a quartet. Over nine years this provided a reasonable part-time income, but what interested Trampler more was the world that was evolving around him, a new world which some of the great composers and musicians were creating. He first met Peggy towards the end of the forties while he was playing with his New Music String Quartet.

Trampler spoke to Peggy of Lake Steinbeck in Munich where he had grown up. He had loved this lake as a child, and although he fought on the American side during the war, its echo was always hauntingly present in his music. Trampler invited Peggy to drinks at his studio loft on 31st Street. Peggy, feeling somewhat hesitant about the handsome young violist, took Anaïs Nin with her. The studio was very impressive, although sparsely furnished, and Anaïs and Peggy tormented Walter with their quick wit and clever anecdotes. Walter said he was flattered to be in the company of such attractive and talented women. He described Peggy as 'very slender and she could smile and come on like a pussy-cat but—you knew she had claws somewhere, hidden'. He described both women as 'alike in personality, strong willed'. 'Anaïs,' he said, 'had the face of an angel but no halo.'

Peggy and Walter met each other at functions and concerts and a friendship began. Walter was impressed with Peggy's music. As a violist it pleased him that she wrote in a contemporary idiom and was interested in instruments. Together they attended jams held at John Cage's studio on the East River, where twice a month composers and musicians would meet to play and perform. It was a place to build understanding between musician and composer. Some of John Cage's string quartet pieces were recorded here. Regulars present at these sessions included John Cage, Milton Babbitt, Henry Cowell, Vladimir Ussachevsky, Otta Luening, Virgil Thomson, Aaron Copland, Colin McPhee and Oliver Daniels (from Broadcast Music Incorporated).

At first anyone working in music was welcome. This changed later when, according to Walter, the gatherings became more select. The group splintered when the Composers' Forum was established with Peggy as director and other groups evolved such as: the Minimalists (the Cage group); the Uptown group and the Downtown group. There was no real opposition among any of these groups and at times crossovers did occur. Walter Trampler, like many other composers and musicians, supplemented his living during the forties by working on commercial jobs such as television, film, and radio performances. Walter remained a friend to Peggy, but it was John Cage she became closer to over time.

In an interview at his New York apartment Cage answered the door to me stark naked. He had a lightweight dressing-gown across his right arm but had not as yet managed to get into it. His mind was full of ideas. He was working on a new piece of music. I stepped into a huge open-space apartment which had trees growing in stoned gardens in the living room. His female secretary was busy looking for things for him, and in the far end of the room behind one of the few partitions was his biographer, apparently one of five such biographers. This charming Italian woman seemed as much a part of his life as one would imagine a neighbour to be. As his biographer she decided to sit in on the interview. John joked in exactly the same way Peggy had done with me, stating that the biographer knows more about one's life story than the subject. 'They're so reliable,' he teased. John Cage was the most lovable of all my interviewees. He invited me to lunch and breakfast on several occasions and was not only a marvellous chef but a brilliant conversationalist. He wanted to talk about everything from the computer age to alienation of the individual in western society, and he wanted fresh opinions. We eventually got round to discussing what I had come for.

Unlike Peggy and most of the others, John Cage was not schooled in the European tradition, and prided himself on *not* having been through Nadia Boulanger's Bakery. Cage's music was considered radical by almost everyone in the musical set, but the likes of Thomson, Copland and Glanville-Hicks were only too happy to have contrary conversation. In Peggy's words, 'John was always full of ideas and beliefs and irregular concepts which he felt could create a music that could converse. A music that would depict the changes. He became famous for his innovative works.'

Peggy and John would experiment with the most unusual of ideas when John was in need of inspiration. During one brainstorming session, Peggy and John put safety pins and pegs in his piano so that it sounded like a harpsichord. John Cage was regarded as the most unorthodox in the group, a position he was loved for. Peggy called him the non-harmonic genius. Peggy described her music to John as being of the modal line, with the adding of rhythm as an accompaniment, especially percussion. 'I feel at home in the modal system and abroad in the diatonic system,' she said. 'And when I told this to Vaugham Williams back in England, he said "Then stay at home". That's what I did.' John mimicked her dialogue cheekily. He laughed in the retelling with a silent husky roar, his trademark according to Peggy. John said he was always amused by Peggy's unexpected intensity. He especially liked her writings. According to Cage, her articles compared music with anything from architecture to cooking, the last analogy being the one she knew least about.

From 1945 to 1955 Cage was at work on a biography of Virgil Thomson. He had also worked as a stringer for him on the *New York Herald-Tribune*, and although they were friends Cage found him extremely difficult. He admired his intellect but was wary of him. On the *Tribune* Cage discovered that Thomson would accept a story submitted from Europe or wherever and then criticise it after publication. Thomson was also disliked for changing an article and not informing or consulting the reviewer. The biography was a constant point of contention during the time John and Peggy were friends. Without his knowledge, she had attempted to persuade Thomson to release Cage from the burden of this biography. Thomson wouldn't budge. He made light of the task he had set Cage, arguing that it was straightforward and that Cage was being precious. Peggy defended Cage. She raised his concerns. Thomson became angry, and in his hostility she came to understand that he regarded it as a debt. She backed off, never telling Cage of the incident.

Musically, 1952 was a big year for Cage, and although he was pained by the Virgil Thomson biography, he managed to attend some of the familiar jam sessions. The composers and musicians were now meeting at Lou Harrison's house to write new music. Some of these impromptu pieces were published as 'party pieces'. Thomson attended with the usual crowd but remained aloof from Cage, which was not easy in such a small gathering.

Peggy had problems accepting some of Cage's more radical music. It seems evident that they could never have combined musical structures. And although they remained good friends, Cage felt that Peggy couldn't take his music seriously. He said she found it 'quite beyond the limits'. This amused rather than angered him and he relished every opportunity to tease her. Peggy liked to write solo and dismissed 'party pieces' as trivial work.

Almost continuously engaged in activities for the propagation of new music and encouragement of new composers, 1943 and 1944 were among Peggy's busiest years. She was active with the League of Composers Committee which was the body that organised concerts in Central Park. It was her ideas and initiative, in collaboration with Dr Carleton Sprague Smith, that founded the International Music Fund. The fund operated through UNESCO and sought to assist artists in postwar re-establishment. Peggy was author of its first manifesto, and on-the-spot reporter for the *Herald-Tribune* at the inaugural benefit concert given at Tanglewood.

She was also at this time a junior member of the Museum of Modern Art. She organised music events of an avant-garde nature for the museum's auditorium, notably: 'The Hispanic Influence in Modern Music' and 'Music for Percussion'— both of these concerts were particularly radical and successful. As part of these concerts she commissioned artists. Carlos Surinach was one such commission. Given free rein to compose, he produced *Tres Cantos Bereberes*. This was a wonderful introduction to American audiences for the Spanish composer, whose reputation had previously been for conducting.

In addition to introducing Surinach, Peggy built a second program around harpist Nicanor Zabaleta, for whom she had written Sonata for Harp. This production established him as a soloist on the American music scene and revived interest in the harp as an instrument for modern composition. Zabaleta also played for Surinach's *Tres Cantos Bereberes*. A reviewer described the harp piece: 'Because the composer regards the tonal security of the harp as fragile, she has eschewed the uncertain anchorage of the contemporary idiom to ensure a tonic feeling and hence a sanctuary as it were, for the deliberately archaic evocation that pervades.'[9]

For the second concert, Peggy wrote her Sonata for Piano and Percussion, which became a standard work in percussion music. The more successful concerts occurred nearer the end of the forties and the beginning of the fifties. In a sense, Peggy enjoyed a double career. One involved activities on behalf of contemporary music, musicians and composers, the second her own musical works. Throughout the forties she produced orchestral pieces, the best known being Dance Cantata which was designed for narrator, spoken chorus and orchestra. In addition she produced some short commercial pieces for film, such as 'Pulsa'—music for a State Department documentary, and a Tel-cartoon piece for Film Graphics Inc.

Her chamber works for voice were equally impressive and included *Five Songs From Housman*, taken from the last poems of the poet A. E. Housman; *Profiles From China*, which was a series of five songs with a vaguely eastern quality; and a popular little chamber vocal piece called *Thirteen Ways of Looking At A Blackbird*. Towards the end of the forties she created *Thomsoniana*, in which she excelled in both wit and genius. The music was set to the words of Virgil Thomson's music reviews. Borrowing from his columns in the *New York Herald-Tribune*, Peggy actually made her championship of the percussion and harp repertoires using this extraordinary text.

The high point of this period for Peggy was the invitation to have her chamber work Concertino da Camera performed at the International Society of Contemporary Music Festival, this time held in Amsterdam. Having been the first Australian composer to be included in such a festival in London ten years earlier, she was now creating musical history with a second inclusion. The Concertino da Camera was designed for clarinet, bassoon and piano, and was recorded the following year by Columbia with pianist Carlo Bussotti performing.

Peggy's financial circumstances had changed and the quality of her life accordingly. The publications to which she contributed extended from the *New York Herald-Tribune* to the *Musical Quarterly*, *Notes*, *Harper's Bazaar*, *Vogue*, *Musical America*, and the *Juilliard Review*. Paul Bowles had left for Tangiers with Jane again during 1945, but spent whatever time he had with Peggy while visiting New York. Stanley now lived mostly in London returning only sporadically to visit Peggy in New York.

The *Australian Herald*[10] wrote of Peggy's involvement in organising open air concerts in New York's Central Park, tracing her success from the summer of 1944–45. A recording of Concertino da Camera was performed on the Australian Broadcasting Commission at this time, and by 1946 she had written over twenty songs for recording. By 1947 she was said to be halfway through her second full length opera, and in that year she completed a work based on the words of a poem entitled 'Monteforte Toledo', specially written for her (in English) by a poet laureate from Guatemala. This piece combined a woodwind orchestra with oboe, gong and a female chorus. On the strength of its success the Guatemalan Conservatorium offered her an appointment to teach with them. Although Peggy was deeply fascinated by the Guatemalan folk music she declined, choosing instead to remain in New York and find her way not as an academic but as a composer.[11] At the same time a second offer of work arrived from Australia which was irresistible.

She was invited by the Australian Broadcasting Commission to give a series of talks on contemporary composers, a topic she relished. She started planning for the visit towards the end of 1948. Doubling up as always, she jointly organised to have an inaugural performance of her music. The work, arranged for narrator, drums and orchestra, was an adaptation from her ballet *Killer and Enemies*, which had been based on a Navajo legend and written specifically for the American dancer Eric Hawkins. Always at work on numerous productions or compositions, she presented to Australian journalists as a highly competent and gifted woman. This was quite a change from the impression, or lack of impression, she had evoked just seven years earlier when resident in Potts Point, Sydney. Australian journalists described her as 'diligent, busy and optimistic beyond belief'.

She was, however, deceptive in one area. When her picture appeared with Stanley Bate she remained silent about the failed marriage. She wanted to avoid scandalous references to her absent husband or herself, though she was known to joke at parties with friends in Sydney that Stanley had in fact 'flown the coop'. She continued to deny his absence publicly, saying that he was away on tour, until their divorce was finalised some ten years later. The romantic caption of June 1947 in the *Australian Herald* depicts Stanley and Peggy as the happy couple. It reads: 'She shall have music wherever she goes.'

The only music Peggy was to enjoy was entirely of her own making and make it she did. She returned to New York after her brief visit to Australia with renewed enthusiasm. As she seated herself in the departing taxi she glanced at the magazine in her hand, the *ABC Weekly*, which was celebrating her music performed by the Melbourne Orchestra. This same magazine introduced a new ABC program, 'Blue Hills', a serial that was to become a nostalgic part of Australia's radio history. She leant forward laughing and tapped the taxi-driver on the back. 'Take me back to the future,' she said, 'and be quick about it, I'm late.'

NOTES

1. Virgil Thomson, *New York Times*, 1942.
2. Ibid.
3. Ibid.
4. *American Composers' Alliance Bulletin*, 1954–55.
5. *American Composers' Alliance Bulletin*, 1955.
6. Held in the State Library of Victoria.
7. Held in the State Library of Victoria.
8. *Diary of Anaïs Nin*, Vol. 5.
9. James Lyons, notes for Long Playing Records, New York.
10. The *Australian Herald*, 9 June 1947.
11. Ibid.

THE
TRANSPOSED HEADS

In June 1948 Peggy appeared for the second time as the Australian representative in the program of the International Society for Contemporary Music. Having made a splash the first time round, she was under pressure to produce something exceptionally good. She was confident.

Like all major arts events there are always joys and disappointments; artists who fail to attend at the last minute due to international politics. This same festival was to be no exception. A sudden change of dates by the International Society for Contemporary Music had made it impossible for a French delegation to attend. The *New Statesman and Nation* reported that 'the presence of a French element in the programs was greatly missed: the element of clarity, lightness, concision and simplicity. Curiously enough, the work most conspicuous for such Gallic virtues came all the way from Australia: a modest and charming Concertino da Camera by Peggy Glanville-Hicks.'

Peggy's former colleague and friend Elisabeth Lutyens represented England in this same festival and her contribution was described in the same article as 'slight in content but quite the most likeable work of this composer'. Lutyens, who was to become a significant composer, had submitted a Horn Concerto.[1]

Reviews of the festival appeared worldwide, and the name Glanville-Hicks appeared in foreign languages in numerous tabloids. Peggy in her methodical way clipped these notices and tucked them away safely until she could have each one translated into English.

The London *Times*'s grave opinion was that:

Composers today are like shipwrecked men struggling in the deep waters of doubt and disillusionment. All around them are floating fragile rafts, at all of which in turn they clutch desperately. Some are labelled 'twelve-tone', others, 'poly-tonal'or 'polyphonic', 'neo-classic' or 'expressionist' but none can offer more than a temporary and precarious foothold or be relied upon to conduct the swimmers to any haven of security where doubts and uncertainty can be supplanted by faith and the pure flame of uninhibited artistic creation.[2]

This particularly conservative article levelled criticism at the diversity of styles, complaining that no one school could be said to predominate. It described the festival as avant-garde and bemoaned the absence of English works. Peggy's work however was described by the journalist as 'pleasing and clever'.

The *New York Times* was much more positive and com-mended the festival for the very things the London *Times* criticised. Peggy's inclusion was described as 'entertaining' and Elisabeth Lutyens' piece as 'original'. The attention from the press inspired Peggy to concentrate solely on her own work, and the 1950s and 1960s proved in some ways the best years of her composing career.

In October 1948 the *New York Herald-Tribune* reviewed Concertino da Camera. Produced this time for the Composers' Forum it was placed with a second work, *Thirteen Ways of Looking at a Blackbird*. It read:

Miss Glanville-Hicks provided a Concertino da Camera that was easy and delightful to listen to and two song cycles that were grateful in range and content to the singing voice. The Concertino well scored for flute, clarinet, bassoon and piano, is in the French serenade tradition of music, aiming simply and unpretentiously at charming, which it does indeed. *Thirteen Ways of Looking at a Blackbird* based on the fine Wallace Stevens poetry seems to experiment with almost as many styles in its piano part as there are segments in the work. This is a healthy sign, for the gracious style of the concertino and her settings of Chinese poems may easily lend itself to facile treatment if pursued too long, and it may be that Miss Glanville-Hicks is now in a transitional stage of

reviewing the many directions open to one today in order
to give greater depth to her creative approach.[3]

The *New York Times* also reviewed other Composers' Forum
productions. It was becoming an impressive showcase under
Peggy's directorship.[4]

Peggy's fascination with putting contemporary poetry to
music continued. In 1951 the musical publication *Notes*
criticised her for this interest, virtually asking her in an article
to turn her attention to less esoteric poetry, less exotic and
fragmentary words as the basis for her work.[5] No doubt they
were referring to the oddity of the text used in *Thirteen Ways
of Looking at a Blackbird*. Being the individual that she was,
she ignored this advice.

Empowered by her small successes, Peggy began to work
long hours at home, often into the early hours of the morning.
Besides reviewing and her work on music boards and associations, her own music had become a priority. She began
making every attempt to get herself included in programs and
planned to produce work for forthcoming musical events as
they came up. At first her offerings were small owing to the
pressure on her time. She submitted works of short length
which demonstrated a high degree of expertise. Her work
began to appear in concerts of contemporary music such as
the Yaddo Music Group in New York, concerts for chamber
music, the Philadelphia Art Alliance music presentation, and
special concerts given in celebration of women composers.
Her music was even produced in Tel Aviv.

Reviews came from all around the world. Small though
these works were, they attracted attention and almost every
production was reviewed. The Concertino da Camera came
to be considered a significant work. The newspapers liked
to photograph composers for the music pages and Peggy's
face now appeared more times than Hindemith's. She also
started to appear in almost as many programs as he did. Her
name came to be associated with other more established
artists. Her music was listed as 'distinguished new work' and

it was widely felt that this P.G.-H. composer had a great deal more to offer.

In 1951 came such songs as *Profiles from China*. Richly endowed harmonically, these small pieces with a variety of rhythmic interest became favourites and appeared as sheet music available for purchase, as did several other compositions. These were followed by other pieces which appeared in the American Music Festival and on radio station WNYC. Reviews in the *New York Herald-Tribune* were predictably favourable. Peggy took exception to the musical publication *Notes*, which had made some generalised criticisms. She made her views known to friends, but did not reproach the publication directly, perhaps because she was writing for them on a part-time basis at the time. She objected to being called a 'newcomer' to music. Some articles claimed incorrectly that *Profiles from China* was a first work for the music critic Glanville-Hicks. On her files at home she wrote comments beside these articles such as 'rubbish' or 'balls'. It was a habit of hers to correct information in books and articles. Irritated by mistakes, be they in content or typographical, she would correct them so that the error would not offend her when next she read it. Even her library of published works bore these corrections.

Late in 1951, *Profiles from China* was performed again, this time by the Juilliard String Quartet in a new program, with Peggy's name alongside Béla Bartók and Haydn. In concerts being performed all over New York City her name recurred in almost every program. These were followed by reviews, and interest in her work continued to grow. In one concert given by the New Music Society Peggy was accompanied by composers Paul Bowles, Virgil Thomson, Lou Harrison, and John Cage.

John Cage shocked audiences with a piece of work he titled *Imaginary Landscape No. 4*, which was written for twelve radios, operated by twenty-four musicians and conducted by the composer, ostensibly in all seriousness, even to the point of loving rubatos for a Beethoven adagio. Reviewed by the

New York Herald-Tribune, Cage's work was described irreverently by journalist Arthur Berger as 'like waiting for a man to be shot from a cannon'. He dismissed the work as 'snatches of broadcasts that are common to the experience of anyone who has twisted a radio dial'. Cage was advised that exponents of such experiments in the 1920s had long since either joined the mainstream, stopped composing or died. Berger went even further in his attack of this avant-garde series. 'The experimentalists [from the 1920s] gloried in invading the machine shop for such devices as anvils, aeroplane propellers and sirens and then . . . have you heard my new concerto for tuba, piccolo, washbasin and alarm clock?'

Not letting any of the other composers escape comment, he next turned to Paul Bowles' Cantata which he said 'seemed to rest largely on the grotesqueness of a harmonium echoing honky-tonk music'. Virgil Thomson was also attacked despite being the chief music editor of the *Tribune* at the time: 'Thomson's *Capital, Capital* opened the group of works and put the audience into a hilarious mood. It too rests on a single idea, the recitative style he evolved for setting Gertrude Stein . . . It becomes wearing on its own for twenty minutes.' Peggy's music was the only piece to escape unscathed.

Berger posed the question, 'Are we to run the risk of being tagged philistine if we ask how serious is some of this music?' He then reverted to his original tone for the final item when, he said: 'Four men arose from the audience, went to the front of the hall, and broadly twirled slabs of wood on strings (thundersticks as they were officially called) to produce a quiet whirring sound to accompany the solemn declamation of a lone cello!'[6] Needless to say, the reviews of this production gained more attention than the production itself.

Virgil Thomson had written a preview to the concert series just two weeks before Berger's review appeared. In Thomson's review John Cage's work is described as:

> An application of the visual arts in music. The composition is by the composer but the textures are borrowed. Picasso,

Marcel Duchamp, Kurt Schwitters and Max Ernst have all worked in this manner using, instead of brush strokes, bits of wallpaper, newspaper, objects of commercial origin, burnt matches, almost anything that is common enough to lack sentimental associations.[7]

Thomson's vision for the concert series was evident in his subheading 'Modernism Goes On'. He re-examined the New York music period of the 1950s.

Today every child is a modernist, there is nothing else to be. His only choice is between the diatonic modern style (known as neoclassic) and the chromatic modern style (commonly referred to as atonal) and these set closer together as the century rolls on. In the old days he could join a variety of sects or none at all. He could even invent one. If he joined nothing, he became an impressionist. Impressionism in the decade following Debussy's death was the reactionary esthetic.

Thomson wanted to make a point that would elevate modernism which, he said,

Is not yet reactionary, though it has become academic. Today's war between liberals and conservatives is being fought out on the box office front, with New York impresarios resisting experiment and restless elements among the artists and the customers agitating for a less rigidly standardised repertory. On the composing front there is no principled war at all. There is only the struggle for place.[8]

Paul Bowles had been with Peggy during these concerts held by the New Music Society. Long conversations ensued as to the future of their relationship. His love of Tangiers, Morocco, and her love of New York meant that separation was inevitable. Jane was not discussed. They both promised to write letters to one another. In many ways it was a sad parting because it was now clear that the relationship would never be more than part-time.

Paul's promise to Peggy led to the creation of a new work, *Letters From Morocco*. Designed for voice and orchestra, this piece of work was based entirely on Paul's letters, in particular his sensitive and poetic descriptions of Tangiers. He had a way of capturing the colour and spiritual atmosphere of the region. One of the amusing lines set to unusually haunting music was: 'I have found a new candy, hashish almond bar! I shall bring you some.' Peggy set this to an exhilarating Moorish tune accompanied by percussion. The text to the opening of No. 3 Suite read: 'There are concerts here too beautiful to imagine, in the Dar Batha.' Two of Peggy's pieces relating this line have an Arabic flavour, the music evoking something of the warming desert winds of Africa.

Letters from Morocco had its first performance at the Museum of Modern Art, in New York in February 1953, with Leopold Stokowski as conductor and Willy Hess as soloist.[9] Its originality had wide appeal and audiences flocked to see it. Paul was overwhelmed by her dedication and their unusual relationship retained its curious continuity, linked by letters and occasional brief visits.

Towards the end of the year, Peggy was scheduled to give a series of university lectures. For these she drew upon her experience as musicologist, composer and critic. The lectures began at the University of Minnesota. Peggy was featured on the front page dailies with headlines: 'The arts in our industrial world by Peggy Glanville-Hicks'. The lectures proved a financial success, paying significantly more than the magazine publications which had funded her other work to date.

Her lectures covered a fascinating assortment of topics, including: Maria Callas—Oracle of the Opera; What Makes an Opera Work?; An Attempt to Investigate Possible Influences of Indian Classical Music on Our Own Music in the Future; and Art and Science as Related Concepts with Discussions by Yehudi Menuhin.

Three additional lectures she gave were intended to form the basis of a book Peggy planned to write, entitled *Apollo's*

House. These lectures were: Climate of Twentieth-Century Music as Architecture; Musical Avant Guardians (which was really a collection of essays on music from 1945 to 1965); and The Contemporary Composer in the Present Day Environment. For someone who had examined and participated in almost every facet of the contemporaneous American music scene these lectures came easily.

Peggy's final lecture about the contemporary composer was particularly interesting. It divided the music scene up into sections. The first was 'Under The Art', referring to the composer's creative process, his–her psychology and how one is to evolve technically and inspirationally. It also addressed financial and spiritual difficulties. The second topic, 'Under The Profession' examined the place composers come to occupy, their influence, both good and bad, on institutions, programs and the like. And the third category, 'In the Trade and Industry', related to the activities undertaken by composers who double as musicians. Various commercial outlets for music such as radio, film, theatre and ballet were also discussed.

The following year there was great excitement when the Louisville Philharmonic Orchestra, funded to the tune of $400,000 from the Rockefeller Foundation, began a search to find and fund some thirty new works. A commissioning committee dispatched invitations to composers all over the world. One such commission arrived on Peggy's doorstep listing her as one of the lucky thirty-nine composers to be asked. The Louisville Philharmonic offered $1,000 for each orchestral commission plus $200 for copying of the parts. It offered $2,000 for an opera with an additional $500 for pieces accepted. Peggy was ecstatic. The *New York Times* outlined what was happening in a November 1953 daily, and heralded the newly-commissioned composers as 'the best'. Fuelled with enthusiasm and belief in herself, Peggy pondered over possible choices for commission, settling eventually on an opera as the supreme challenge! It would take several months just to research and submit her plans.

Work continued as usual on the *Tribune*. Although she was said to be an established and respected music critic, Peggy hadn't noticed that she had grown up as a critic. Throughout the ten years or so that she had worked with the paper she had always regarded other critics as superior. She felt she lacked something as a reviewer. She hadn't begun life as a journalist and suspected there was some mystery she was yet to unravel. Still quoted in America as recently as the 1980s, it is difficult to understand where this feeling of inferiority came from. Publicly she was proud to be a critic. She was combative and precise, ready to defend her views with anyone. Only privately did she cringe about the art of journalism. The only hint of this hidden fear of inadequacy was the praise she lavished on other critics.

One of New York's oldest organisations, the Composers' Forum was undergoing a major crisis when Peggy joined in 1950. Funding had been a problem for a number of years and activities had slowed dramatically. But in the fall of 1951 a Miss Jean Tennyson, who was a member of a large family of philanthropists, gave the organisation a new lease of life by funding it over a three-year period. Jean Tennyson was famous for her funding of Artist Veterans, which was a company of famous entertainers who performed for men in army hospitals.

The Forum had enjoyed government sponsorship during the 1930s but the value of its assets had declined and it lost its venue. A permanent home was found at Columbia's McMillin Theatre with the joint sponsorship of Columbia University and the Music Department of the New York Public Library. Some sponsorship came from a fund known as the Alice Ditson Fund. But its assets remained modest, and with the arrival of Peggy Glanville-Hicks as director and adequate funding from Tennyson, it became possible to pay performers and composers for their contributions and to expand the Forum's sphere of operations. Peggy was in her element. She loved to organise events and people.

The 1950s was a hectic decade for Peggy. As director of the Composers' Forum, she organised seven concerts each year, many of which were designed for young composers to make their musical debut. Peggy's primary aim was to set up concerts and achieve follow-up recordings. She did this within the first two years, and more than a dozen major works were recorded. Some of these recordings were of music that had been professionally performed before. They included revivals such as *Ballet Mécanique* by George Antheil, and the Concerto for Piano and Wind Octet by Colin McPhee. Paul Bowles' opera *The Wind Remains* was also amongst them. Some of these works had remained buried for twenty years. Peggy saw value in combining mature work with new work, and in her opening speech as director declared: 'We must embrace a notion that the creating of channels of opportunity for the creative musician is a privilege, a duty and a challenge of vital importance, and one of perpetually recurring pressure and need in each generation.'

She also set up a reading committee which included Henry Cowell, Otto Luening and any other colleague or willing composer who would act as a talent scout and participate in the committee for the purposes of advancing the career paths of young composers. A high standard of technical efficiency and aesthetic judgement was the only prerequisite for being on this committee. Many a great composer became a part of the committee during its heyday and it was hoped that such a platform might again be resurrected.[10]

The debutante concerts, as Peggy called the performances of new composers, became quite successful. Although programmed with the mature composers' work, all new work received special attention. Several selections were taken from each new composer's work, performed, then examined before an audience and a forum. The forum consisted of a panel of composers with Peggy in centre position as compere and critic. The audiences were invited to write their questions down on a piece of paper and these were then forwarded to Peggy to read out; the composers and critics answered in turn. One evening John Cage was in the audience and as a joke sent up a piece of paper which asked, 'Is there life on Mars?' Peggy read out the question in all seriousness. There was hilarious laughter throughout the hall. She suddenly recognised the handwriting and announced over the microphone, 'If Mr Cage is there would he kindly leave the room.' And he did.

Peggy's composition work continued to grow during the 1950s and the rewards began to pour in. In 1953 she won an American Academy of Art and Letters scholarship for composition, followed in 1956–57 by two Guggenheim fellowships. In 1957–58 she received a Fulbright Fellowship for music research. With the financial security these grants gave she was able to devote long stretches of uninterrupted time to composing. She all but retired from her position on the *New York Herald-Tribune*, doing only part-time reviews that appealed to her. She began to discriminate between working commitments so as to make room for her own composition. She was eager to get started on the commissioned opera.

The commission from the Rockefeller Foundation for the Louisville (Kentucky) Orchestra was $4,000. On submission of an outline stating that she would base her opera on a work by the German author Thomas Mann (a novel of life on the Jumna River in India), the foundation organised ahead for an American network to televise the opera and for a commercial recording program. Her introductory submission had clearly overwhelmed the judges at the foundation, and provided great excitement in the Louisville Philharmonic.

The director of the Philharmonic Orchestra, Moritz Bomhard, met her to go over the details of the commission. Newspapers across the country and at home in Australia reported the story of the commission, and she was under pressure to meet the deadline with a work of brilliance. This was the opportunity she had been waiting for. Miraculously she managed to extricate herself from other commitments and set off for Port Antonio, Jamaica, to work.

She was to be the guest of Theodore Flynn, a former professor of zoology at Sydney University, who was running a hotel in Port Antonio. An experienced oceanographer, Theodore had met Peggy on several occasions, and they shared a nostalgic tie with Australia. Within days of her arrival, however, Peggy found the hotel too noisy for work and decided to look for a cottage. Theodore found her the ideal house on the outskirts of town, quiet, and set at the edge of a cliff. Surrounded by a large veranda, it had an Australian flavour. Peggy was delighted with it.

In the evenings the two would sometimes meet for dinner and talk about their former lives in Australia. On weekends, wearing a straw hat and a bikini, Peggy would climb down the cliff to the beach below to swim in the rock pools. The natural formation of the rock pools made it possible to swim from one rock pool to another by catapulting through a sluice pool. Theodore was an expert at this, and he and Peggy spent a good part of the day swimming and sunning themselves. New York seemed far away.

Theodore would arrive early every Saturday morning loaded up with fresh vegetables and fruit from Port Antonio. The salutatory bottle of wine was always reason enough for Peggy to abandon her composition and take to the beach. She described this time with Theodore as 'being Aussies together'. Theodore always referred to her simply as P.G., and she admitted that if he'd been twenty years younger he'd have been close to being the perfect mate for her. As a result of this friendship, Peggy had an incidental meeting with the actor Errol Flynn, who was Theodore's son.

A ferocious storm blew up one weekend while Peggy was living in Port Antonio. The roads were washed away by floods, and food supplies and petrol were cut off. Telephone lines were down, and contact with neighbouring homesteads cut. Theodore became worried and set out with Errol in his vehicle to rescue Peggy. They arrived at Peggy's cottage and were relieved to find her safe and well. The rain had penetrated the house, ruining a few household items and the roof was leaking, but Peggy had not entertained the idea of leaving. She was halfway through an opera!

While Theodore and Errol were there the rain fell even harder, washing out the road and a small bridge and they were forced to stay the night. It was a joyful dinner with P.G. and Theodore chatting good-humouredly, their mutual laughter rising up over the dinner table as they shared stories and intrigues. Errol was charming and well-mannered but a little restless about the flood waters. Later that evening Peggy played some of her compositions at the piano cheered on by Theodore. Theodore retired leaving Peggy and Errol to drink cocoa on the front veranda.

Together they watched the storm. The conversation was personal at times and Errol asked many intimate questions. Peggy felt an absence in his response. She later described him as a 'spirit without a soul'. Errol had none of the ease and humour of his father, and was unhappy in life generally. She perceived in him an interminable restlessness that bordered on grief.

The storm eventually subsided and Errol and his father drove back to town the next afternoon. When Errol said goodbye, he held Peggy's hand for a moment and stared at her. She thought he had felt understood. This moment had made her feel sad; his emptiness had returned. Errol and Peggy never saw each other again, but several years later he sent her a postcard with respectful congratulations when a recording of hers was released.

At the end of four months, Peggy emerged with the script of an opera to be titled *The Transposed Heads*. George Antheil wrote a complete breakdown of the script in the *American Composers' Alliance Bulletin* after interviewing her.

The story is like other books by Thomas Mann, a miraculous blend of realistic drama and metaphysical discourse. For the realist, the story goes something like this. A young Brahmin, Shridaman and his low-caste friend, Nanda, while resting in a forest glade are inadvertently the witnesses of the ritual bathing of a lovely young maiden, Sita, who comes to the river bank. Shridaman, the ascetic, without realising it, becomes an immediate victim of her voluptuousness. Meeting some days later Nanda finds his young friend dying from love and despair. He laughs at him and promises to woo and win the lovely Sita on his friend's behalf, according to Hindu custom.

The wedding scene is wholly joyful, but tragedy comes swiftly thereafter. The three, while journeying through a forest, come upon an immense ruined Temple of Kali, and Shridaman leaves Sita and Nanda together while he enters to say a prayer. It is immediately apparent that there is unspoken love blossoming between the wife and the friend. Shridaman, inside the temple is overcome with awe and religious fervour as he contemplates the gigantic Kali and, momentarily hypnotised by her power, offers himself as a sacrifice, cutting off his own head with a sword. Nanda, following to find his friend, sees the disaster, blames himself and his secret love for Sita, and follows suit, beheading himself beside his friend. Next comes Sita to discover the double tragedy, and she, also blaming herself for her unfaithfulness, in mind at least, to her husband, prepares to hang herself in a trailing vine, when Kali's immense voice is heard.

The Goddess, after chiding Sita for her stupidity, instructs her to place the heads back on, promising that all will be again as it was. Sita, in fear and trembling, performs the bloody task, but in her flurry she makes the Freudian slip of all time, and places the husband's head upon the lover's body, and vice versa. They rise up, irrevocably transposed, and who is now to say which is the legal husband, which the friend.

A Guru is consulted and proclaims the head as the rightful husband. Sita should surely have been content but no. After time passes she begins to pine for the other parts, the Nanda head and the husband body, and presently she can bear it no longer, and sets out to find him in his hermit's retreat. Shridaman has followed her and the three, united again in the impossible triangle, decide that there is no solution but to merge all their separate essences in the universal whole by jumping into the flames. Accordingly a funeral pyre is built, but it is not permitted that a wife commit suicide until she is a widow; so Nanda and Shridaman fight a duel, piercing each other to the heart in a single moment and as they fall upon the fire, Sita steps in beside them and all are consumed.

Mann's story in its higher octave was a curious blend of typical Hindu thought and his own philosophical manner as he continually touched upon the metaphysical laws of balance, the pairs of opposites, as the Hindu called the universal laws that cause attraction, repulsion, completion and poise, and in which human lives and loves on earth become so torn and tangled.[11]

Peggy was entranced with the story. She felt it contained all the qualities she strove for in her music, and that she could be experimental with the music. She could combine Indian folk elements with melody–rhythm, and bring eastern and western nuances together, a theme that had long persisted at the edges of her work. She also enjoyed the 'wickedness' as she put it, the drama of a woman caught between two men. She loved, too, Mann's language; it made an ideal libretto.

The Transposed Heads is both rambunctious and lilting. The music rises and falls, returns to the moment of poise and completion. Like the libretto, it plays on opposing themes and emotions. It screams and whispers. It could be Indian within Western music, or the reverse. Never careless in structure, the form is controlled yet unexpected. It evokes the Indian world, a serenity within the centre of the storm.

The first performance of *The Transposed Heads* took place on 4 April 1954, and was heralded as the first major operatic event of such magnitude to occur in Louisville. One review began, 'Beyond any doubt, the premiere of *The Transposed Heads* was a successful one. The audience embraced it enthusiastically at the final curtain, and recalled singers, director and composer to the stage repeatedly until the house lights went on.'[12] A second review spoke of 'a lucid fantasy framed in melodious music' and the use of 'exotic rhythms and authentic Hindu music to tell a story of a tragic triangle.'[13] Moritz Bomhard (director of the Louisville Philharmonic) was quoted praising the score for its frequent passages of melodic beauty and for the fact that the composer had written music that was always sympathetic to the human voice. He said 'the large group of percussion instruments (Chinese gongs and the like) added to the regular orchestra gives the score a strange, exotic dignity.'[14]

Friends of Peggy told me of an affair she had with the charming Moritz Bomhard. Peggy herself never wanted to tell much about him during the writing of the biography. Perhaps she was embarrassed by the affair. Her own diaries indicate that he was more important to her than was allowed to be known. In his position it could easily be misconstrued that he used his position to get her the commission. In fact the two had never really talked until the production was under way. Quarrels, arrivals and partings indicated in her diaries show the liaison was disastrous. It also seems to have been fuelled by musical enthusiasm. The entries read: 'Moritz flew home, no word why? We quarrel. Moritz leaves for Brussels. Ah but the music! Mailed letter. Three weeks since saw Moritz. Moritz returns. I am returning his letters.'

Over the next two weeks she writes in big bold letters, 'THINK, Think, THINK. Dinner with Moritz'. She draws a little star throughout the diaries to indicate consummation, the moment of splendour, the actual night. Moritz features in star formation throughout these weeks. Near the end of the affair, some weeks pass, the bold words appear again. 'THINK, think, THINK' and then Moritz disappears from the pages of the diary forever.

She described him with detachment in later years as 'a

disciplined, passionate man who had made his way to become director of the Louisville Philharmonic Orchestra by dedication and perseverance'. He no doubt recognised in Peggy a musicologist his equal. This artistic and astute woman was everything he could ever have imagined, but in a short time he realised that, like himself, Peggy could not be bullied and pushed around. 'He didn't know how to cope with a woman as competent as himself,' said Peggy, and so what had flowered as a wildly passionate meeting of twin souls collapsed.

Favourable reviews for *The Transposed Heads* continued to arrive following its New York opening. A review by popular music critic Robert Evett, and another which appeared in *World Theatre*, published by the International Theatre Institute, intimated that Peggy Glanville-Hicks was going to be a composer of long-term significance.

The New York production met with only one really bad review. In true form, Peggy promptly wrote the reviewer a stiff note suggesting that next time he stay for the second half.

Peggy always had a story to tell, and she saved the Thomas Mann story until after the production opened. The critics were more than pleased to have snippets about the famous author. Peggy had written to Thomas Mann shortly after beginning work on *The Transposed Heads* asking his approval. 'Do you remember me, the "long legged composer"?' she began. They had met in previous years at occasional literary events, long before Peggy had the idea of writing the libretto.

He was pleased to hear from her, and happy to have her adapt the work so long as it did not involve him. But as the project progressed, he became more interested. Peggy decided that she would simply underline the text she required without much alteration and send drafts for his approval. He replied promptly. Telling her, ironically, that he had always been interested in the combination of words and music, he made suggestions as to how to extract value from the language. Complimenting him on his choice, Peggy indicated the areas best suited to aria and recitative. Mann became fascinated, drafts ran hot in the mail, and in no time the libretto took shape. Sometimes Mann would send one letter after another with hints on how to fine-tune the text.

Mann was taken ill some time before the final draft of the opera was finished and could not attend the opening night. He wrote from his hospital bed in Switzerland, asking that a copy of the recording be sent. Unfortunately the recording arrived on the day he died.

A few months after the production, while visiting India, Peggy was asked to give an introductory speech on *The Transposed Heads* for All Radio Broadcast. In this speech she addressed the dilemma of Western music. In some way this introduction served as an explanation of her musical views. *The Transposed Heads* had provided her with what she termed 'the first synthesis of her ideas'.

Western composition technique and esthetic is to my mind at an impasse. The advent of the keyboard and the tempered scale just before Bach's time made available vertical duplication of notes in chords, this in turn giving rise to the orchestra. Came the classic, then the romantic eras, with the vertical focus, the harmonic aspect, becoming more and more the main preoccupation of composers. Romanticism passed in due course to impressionism, with composers such as Debussy and Scriabin making the harmonic clusters almost the sole consideration. Our own time saw this whole harmonic edifice topple into a chaos of dissonance where the formula of Schoenberg and the formalism of later Stravinsky sought to bring order by intellectual tenet. I was myself a graduate of both these dissonant schools, but a conviction grew that melody and rhythm were the basic, perennial structural and expressive elements in music, that in harmony or the vertical concept Western music had come to the end of the line. Accordingly, some years ago I threw out harmony, and with it of course went dissonance, a step that appeared to enrage some of my avant garde contemporaries who regarded me as some kind of traitor to the modernistic cause!

I added a great deal of percussion, to build up the rhythm section, and gradually there evolved a melody–rhythm kind of structure that was, I began to realise, getting quite close in concept to the musical patterns of Indian music which I had loved for half a lifetime as a thing apart from my own tradition. When one loves something very deeply, one wants to remove everything that stands between oneself and that thing. I loved the purity and joyousness of the music of India— particularly the folk tunes and dances—and in using actual Indian melodies and fragments in *The Transposed Heads*, I wanted to capture those moods and bring them to the West uninfringed in their intrinsic nature. I wanted to find a way of creating—as it were—direct from the nature of that material, shedding all other technical and esthetic preconceptions, and letting the material re-create me in its own image.[15]

In the late fifties Peggy wrote a number of articles on Western composition. It seemed to her inevitable, in view of modern communications media, that Western music and its instruments were going to penetrate Asia, and that the creative artists in both East and West had to take hold of the situation and steer the cross-fertilisation toward a positive and beautiful result. To this end, and also because of the relevance of India's musical theory to the Western situation, it became her greatest ambition to journey to India and make a deeper study of the subject. Visits to India were therefore intermittently included in her schedule.

Peggy's personal life had taken a few unexpected turns. With Paul Bowles in Tangiers more than in New York, it looked seriously as if work had won out over attachment. Her relationship to Stanley Bate, caught up in his own life and work, was a tenuous one. He displayed little interest in Peggy during his visits from London. To say they were close friends, as some did, is an overstatement, although they were occasionally seen out drinking together and discussing music. Despite everything Peggy never lost respect for Stanley as a composer. She remained encouraging and proud of his achievements. The same could not be said of him. His opinion of his wife's work is unknown. Stanley and Peggy ceased living together within the first two to four years of their arrival in New York, yet Peggy continued to cite Stanley as next-of-kin in passports and yearly address books. His address noted in her diary during his visits indicates that he stayed within one block of her apartment.

The separation had been a logical step for a relationship that had become more that of brother and sister than of an equal partnership between lovers. Months passed between their meetings, and in a way the relationship loss was felt less because of the ambiguity of the situation. This state of affairs would have continued indefinitely had Stanley not decided to ask for a divorce.

There are many versions of their divorce. Peggy said that Stanley was in need of a sponsor, and had taken up with Margarida Nogueora or Maggs as she was affectionately known. Maggs had met the estranged couple during Peggy's production of *The Transposed Heads*, but they had also met some years before during the performance of Peggy's Sonata for Harp played by Nicanor Zabaleta. Perhaps Maggs knew of Peggy's attachment to Paul Bowles. Peggy certainly knew of her affection for Stanley. It seems there was a convivial friendship between them. Maggs, according to Peggy, was the acting Brazilian Ambassador in New York, but this might simply have meant that she was a dignitary of some stature from Brazil. A wealthy and capable woman, Margarida persuaded Stanley to return to Brazil with her where she offered to arrange appearances and performances for him.

Stanley was interested in tours of any sort and would have found this an attractive proposition professionally. He did visit Brazil with Margarida, and after two months she arranged a musical tour not only of Brazil but of Europe. When the tour ended Stanley returned to London with Margarida. He rang Peggy to push his plans for divorce, perhaps prompted by Margarida. Peggy complied with his wishes, believing Margarida to be the better sponsor, or so she said, but it is unlikely that she relinquished her marriage to Bate without some degree of pain. Even in New York, divorce in the fifties was an ugly experience.

There was speculation that Margarida and Stanley were to marry but, according to Peggy, Margarida didn't wait until the wedding night to discover her talented lover's sexual preference. Realising Stanley's homosexuality, she dropped him. Stanley was deeply grieved, suggesting that the relationship with Margarida was significant for him. He was found dead in his hotel room weeks after the failure of his intended second marriage, having taken an overdose. There was a great deal of gossip concerning his true intention. Peggy claimed Stanley was a regular user of sleeping pills and believed he had mistakenly overdosed. Margarida considered it an act of suicide.

Peggy was thrown into a state of utter grief. With divorce separating them only months before his death, the rejection was twofold. Peggy cancelled all bookings, meetings, concerts and activities and took to her bed for several days. In her diaries she entered on each page, 'Think, think, think', just as she had written earlier during her affair with Bomhard. Although lovers and relationships had come and gone since their marital separation, for Peggy some essential bond remained unbroken. There was no role for her to play in his death. She was not the loved one of the moment, nor the sister, although she knew this role well. She was the forgotten friend despite having once been his wife and colleague. Burial arrangements were dealt with in London. There was a simple ceremony which Peggy was unable to attend.

Rising out of her shock, she made rigorous efforts to ensure that Stanley's musical scores be gathered and preserved. This took several months, numerous phone calls to London and Europe, numerous letters, meetings and discussions. At the end of this period Peggy had successfully collected and stored almost all of the Bate scores. Her loyalty was spent.

NOTES

1. *The New Stateman and Nation*, 26 June 1948.
2. London *Times*, June 1948.
3. *New York Herald-Tribune*, 25 Oct. 1948.
4. *New York Times*, 25 Oct. 1948.
5. *Notes*, Sept. 1951.
6. *New York Herald-Tribune*, 20 May 1951.
7. *New York Herald-Tribune*, 6 May 1951.
8. *New York Herald-Tribune*, 6 May 1951.
9. *New York Herald-Tribune*, 22 Feb. 1953
10. Peggy Glanville-Hicks, 'Composers' Forum', *American Composers' Alliance Bulletin*, 1950s.
11. *American Composers' Bulletin*, Vol. IV, no. 1, 1954.
12. William Mootz, the Louisville *Courier Journal*.
13. The *Louisville Times*, 5 April 1954.
14. The Louisville *Courier Journal*, 28 March 1954.
15. Peggy Glanville-Hicks' notes, State Library of Victoria.

ONLY
ONE STANDARD

Peggy had always taken a keen interest in folk music from countries such as India and Africa. She wanted to know the sounds and range of every musical instrument known to humankind, as well as those newly invented by eccentrics. As part of the board of the Junior Council of the Museum of Modern Art, she and Paul Bowles, during one of his visits from Tangiers, set up a program entitled Music For Percussion. They included in the program 'their boss man' (as Peggy loved to call him) Virgil Thomson, as well as Carlos Surinach, Elliott Carter and Henry Cowell.

Both Peggy and Paul shared a love of percussion instruments. Peggy felt percussion to be much underrated, saying that too often it was the lemon in the tea or the sauce on the steak. This program aimed to prove that percussion music could have far greater meaning. The result was highly successful and heavily reviewed by a number of daily newspapers.

Comments ranged from, 'few musicians are held in such awe as an orchestral percussion player' to 'there was no meat to it, and very little nourishment'.[1] Both comments oddly enough made by the same journalist for the same publication, yet written on separate nights. The *New York Times* was extremely positive, heralding Carlos Surinach as a 'brilliant' composer. One musical publication zeroed in on Peggy's work for being a 'blank', describing her Sonata for Piano and Percussion as suffering from faulty acoustic planning. Its texture, described as lumpy, failed to 'coalesce into a persuasive sound'. 'Moreover, the melodic–harmonic ideas awarded to the piano are not out of Miss Glanville-Hicks' top drawer, and suggest rather too much the Bedouins-in-the-desert and rush-hour-in-Hong-Kong traditions?' In cowardly fashion, this piece was initialled C.S.[2] No doubt the challenge would have been on had she known the identity of the reviewer.

The *United Press Red Letter* was a full-page liftout inserted in a variety of leading newspapers in the fifties. It was a type of news feature page, an entertainment press release. Journalist Paul Mocsanyi interviewed Peggy on percussion music in this column under the heading 'Schoenberg Old Hat and So's Atonality To Percussionists'. Much of what she had to say indicates her cheekiness. It also indicates her social role as 'speaker for the boys' as well as some of her more serious views about where percussion was situated in her own music.

'Our music was initiated twenty years ago by Henry Cowell and Edgard Varèse, Paul Bowles, Lou Harrison, John Cage, Colin McPhee and Alan Hovhaness—they are our other leaders. The percussionists want to change music entirely,' explained Peggy. 'Melody, already on the wane since the days of atonality, is completely disregarded. They consider harmony a "dated decorative device". Their music consists of rhythm and nothing but rhythm. The exclusion of melody and harmony is but part of the percussion program. Another thing is the elimination of the tempered scale which has been the musical alphabet of Western civilisation for the last three hundred years. European music was, after all, a detour,' she ended amusingly.

It is difficult to know exactly what first drew Peggy to an interest in percussion instruments, but she would have been exposed to a range of cultures in her travels. Paul Bowles would also have had an influence, and certainly John Cage, whom Peggy saw a lot of during these years, did much to consolidate her views in the area of percussion. It is interesting to note that Peggy never used any Aboriginal instruments in her work. It would appear that Australia had little respect for its native music during the years Peggy was growing up. It was certainly never discussed with any seriousness in the musical institutions that she attended.

In the early fifties several of Peggy's works received critical acclaim: *Ballade*, which consisted of three songs for voice and piano, the text from poems written by Paul Bowles; *Pastoral*, written for women's chorus and English horn; and *Thomsoniana*, five musical parodies for tenor or soprano with flute, horn, piano and string quartet. In subsequent performances *Thomsoniana* earned a number of reviews, such as Jay S. Harrison's for the *New York Herald-Tribune*: 'As music they are rich in sentiment as a hymnal and as direct and full of meaning as a pistol shot. The audience response to them was immediate and prolonged.'[3] *Thomsoniana* also earned reviews from publications such as the *Colorado Springs Gazette*, claiming that 'The audience loved the work.'[4] Virgil Thomson hearing this wrote in the *New York Herald-Tribune* three weeks later that, 'the Stravinsky comment is pointed, the Satie homage imaginative, the Schoenberg burlesque—ending with a realistic horse laugh on the cello—riotously funny.'[5]

Another re-performed work from this period, Sonata for Harp, also drew attention. It appeared in several programs and did much to advance the career of the Spanish harpist Nicanor Zabaleta. It was played in venues such as the Museum of Modern Art, and in two other programs when Peggy shared the stage with colleagues Henry Cowell, Virgil Thomson, Carlos Surinach (who was later to become involved in another major opera of Peggy's) and Paul Bowles. Zabaleta even toured with the piece to England where a program of harp pieces included the works of Bach, Beethoven and Hindemith. In the late 1980s Peggy's piece received an award for 'the greatest contribution to harp music' from Pittsburgh, accompanied by a cheque for $2000. A remarkable feat for a piece of music made famous thirty year earlier.

With her continued success the name Peggy Glanville-Hicks was found in every contemporary music event, neatly tucked in beside the giant composers of the century. This was exactly what Peggy had always wanted.

George Antheil, American composer and journalist, wrote an article on Peggy for the *American Composers' Alliance*

Bulletin which featured a photograph of her on the front cover. It began:

> I once thought: music is an art form that requires too great a tensile strength from moment to moment to produce great women composers. Then I began to wonder whether women were by nature serious enough, persevering enough, about a vastly technical art like music, to knuckle down and learn this gigantic discipline.

He went on to say,

> Peggy Glanville-Hicks can never be reproached on technical grounds. I hardly know of a composer working today who has, from every point of view a better technique, both in the handling of musical substances and in their instrumentation. By this I do not mean only that the academic background is beyond criticism; for she has long since assimilated the laws, and discarded the rules of the game.[6]

Despite the praise, and Peggy's strength of opinion in asserting herself as a composer, it was articles such as this which irritated her most. She feared that if composers were separated by gender then the women would be relegated to a women's arena, and this would ultimately mean their invisibility. In this very article Antheil anticipates her opinion of his story by including her much used statement 'there is only one standard to be met, the top one. Given this standard, sex is of no more relevance than is the colour of hair, skin or eyes among male composers.' Peggy was also quick to correct racist statements where they appeared. She believed that in America she had found a more tolerant and advanced society where inequality was becoming a thing of the past.

In Australia an embarrassing white Australia policy had ceased to find support, and immigration policies were amended to actively encourage migration. In America Martin Luther King was emerging as the leader of a campaign for desegregation. Leonard Bernstein was becoming a household name and many other friends of Peggy's such as Yehudi

Menuhin, Benjamin Britten and Gian Carlo Menotti were already famous. On another musical scale Elvis Presley was gaining popularity. And in New York, Maria Callas, the soprano singer, made her debut in Bellini's *Norma* at the Metropolitan Opera. Peggy made a note of this detail in her diary and set plans in motion to include Callas in a work of her own at a later date. At the 1955 International Society for Contemporary Music Festival held in West Germany, Australian composer Peter Sculthorpe's Piano Sonatina was performed. Peggy began to follow his career enthusiastically, combing the newspapers and musical quarterlies. Twenty years later they were to become neighbours and friends. The year 1956 saw the foundation of the Elizabethan Theatre Trust Opera Company, the first nationally-funded Australian opera company. Its first season was an all-Mozart program. This news and more flooded into Peggy's mailbox.

In New York a radio series called 'This I believe' captured something of these times. Published also as a weekly newspaper feature, it attempted to present the personal philosophies of 'Thoughtful Men and Women in All Walks of Life'. What emerged from the readings was an individual view, optimistic of societal change but hindered by the morality of the former decade. The editor invited Peggy to participate. Her contribution, a surprisingly philosophical one, appeared quite soon after. It said:

> I believe that there is a set of infallible laws operating throughout the universe, which maintain poise; poise being the point of balance and integration that ensures eternal continuity.
>
> These laws encompass everything we know, and extend far beyond what we know—or can know, preserving their same quality and infallibility. They are manifest cosmically in the most abstract way, applying also to the human nature in matters of ethical morality, justice, and other factors inherent in human beings and which are above purely rational explanation.

I believe that what we know as the good, the whole, the healthful, are manifestations existing in accord with these laws or this comprehensive Truth; the bad, the divided and distintegrating, the destructive—are momentary deviations, a misapplication or false channelling of its enormous power, which, in itself is neutral, and can be used by us for our own health of the spirit, or its death.[7]

This lengthy document went on to expound the virtues of keeping within the universal laws. It also explored concepts of time and motion, the concern of other art forms and intellectual groups of the period. The author Lawrence Durrell, whom Peggy read, was not alone in his exploration of these themes. There were hints of Einstein's theory of relativity and, in particular, spatial relationships, but Peggy's preoccupation with higher truth sounded less like the philosophy of the day and more in keeping with her Church of England upbringing. It was a time of soul-searching for Peggy, who had risen from Melbourne, Australia, to become a household name in New York.

She had recently written a series of three songs which became extremely popular. They were titled *Gymnopedie No. 1* for oboe, harp and strings; *No. 2* for harp, celeste and strings, and *No. 3* for harp and strings. These songs were surprisingly romantic and played constantly by radio stations. Two reviews appeared which examined the impact of these songs. 'They are peaceful and restful, eminently so-slow, wandering vagrant melodies with throbs of rhythms in the background'[8] and: 'The music itself is strong and muscular, it echoes of Satie. It is remarkably melodic and filled with musical figures that return to the memory persistently.'[9]

The songs had great commercial value. Peggy recalled taking a taxi and hearing them. When she entered a restaurant that same evening she heard the music again. She discovered to her horror that in one establishment a toilet seat, when raised, played the *Gymnopedie*. They were an overwhelming success.

Peggy was convinced she had set enough work in motion to retreat from the many concerts she was still engaged in organising and to retreat from the numerous requests for articles to rethink her next direction. Armed with a Guggenheim scholarship she decided she would travel for one year to write another opera.

Peggy travelled extensively during the following year. First she went to California, to the home of Yehudi Menuhin, where she helped Yehudi restore a recently-discovered Mozart manuscript for a performance he was to give. She fell in love with a young musician who was working with Yehudi at the time. 'This passionate affair was fast and sweet and ended just in time for Peggy to catch her plane to the melodic South,' Peggy said.

She was next invited to open a new music venue in India by the Gandhi family. It seemed a suitable arrangement, as she had plans to visit Australia. 'India,' she said, 'always revived her musically and spiritually.' In her major work of this period she was attempting to shift away from Indian influences and think instead of ancient civilisations: the Greeks, the Romans, the Etruscans. She had hopes of spending time with her friend Indira Gandhi to discuss this shift. Instead, she was taken on a host of interesting tours and spoke only briefly with Indira over lunch during her ten-day stay. Indira was busy at work and her political duties seemed more pressing than the composer's search for inspiration, so Peggy hurried on to Australia.

Her mother died while Peggy was en route. Peggy was deeply grieved. She imagined that her mother had thought her a failure for not having achieved financial independence. She felt success in the musical sense had been expected of her, that it had been the only thing that would make sense of her mother's generous patronage. Peggy's diaries indicate that financial and material support had continued throughout her adult years. There are even entries of money received from

Australia during her marriage to Stanley Bate. The detailed financial planning found at the back of each yearly diary indicates that Peggy had become reliant on this modest financial assistance from home. Peggy could not believe that her mother loved her, despite Myrtle's continued financial support and despite her brother Beric's insistence.

Somewhere in Peggy's imaginings she saw her mother as duty-bound, looking after the only child who couldn't make it financially on her own, who hadn't married well. Peggy perceived the relationship as complicated. She had written to her mother of every concert, performance and newspaper clipping. Perhaps her mother had ceased to reply to her letters. Whatever the details, when Peggy returned to her mother's home after her death she was thrilled to discover that her mother had kept every letter she had ever sent her. There at the bottom of the dresser drawers, tied up in yellow ribbon, was Peggy's success story. This was a surprising revelation to Peggy.

Perhaps there had been some incident between mother and daughter that no-one spoke of? Peggy's sense of distance from her mother was unfathomable. After her initial excitement at finding the letters, her grief returned anew. Her mother had left an inheritance especially for her, but this also failed to convince her of the absent love. Perhaps she was always trying to measure up, to make her mother proud, and secretly resented the dependency it brought. Yet Peggy had appointed her mother as guardian angel in her life, claiming to have heard her mother's voice on numerous occasions, which usually came to impart some warning of danger. Curiously, the voice never appeared during a celebration of success. Peggy was pleased with her mother's spiritual visits but disappointed that 'sometimes there were gaps of years between one utterance and another'.

It may be that Peggy's perception of her mother's qualities made her feel inadequate. She would describe her as 'handsome in a way I am not' or 'strong and powerful in a unique way, distant, not being one to show her feelings'. She never described her as loving and kind, Myrtle had never been the affectionate mother that Peggy longed for. Peggy was relieved to have escaped motherhood. Perhaps she doubted her own ability to give warmth, or perhaps the relationship between mother and daughter was not something she wanted to repeat.

Interviewed by the Melbourne *Age*, the *Sun* and the *Argus* during her winter visit to Australia in 1952, she displayed a keen interest in helping other young artists succeed as she had done. She offered open assistance to any young Australian composer who desired to have their material heard in the US. This was no light offer and in the years that followed she assisted every promising young composer who arrived on her doorstep or wrote to her. She gave journalists detailed instructions as to how young Australian composers might finance themselves—suggesting publication, or individual money collections for concerts. The newspapers cheered her as a major talent.

During these wanderings she did in fact complete an opera, and returned to New York with a performance scheduled at the YWHA Concert Hall on 14 May 1954. Reviewed by the *Musical Times*,[10] *The Glittering Gate* was another success. It was essentially a comedy in one act. Based on a play by Lord Dunsany, the story was about two burglars outside the gates of heaven. One retains his safe-cracking instrument with which he succeeds in opening the gate, only to find a sky full of stars. A simple but well-produced, well-cast mini-opera, the production pleased Peggy but somehow wasn't challenging or meaningful enough.

She had also spent the previous twelve months experimenting with music for ballet, and on her holiday away had written an orchestral piece titled *Etruscan Concerto*. Peggy had been interested in archaeology and ancient history since her summer courses at Oxford. Of particular interest to her were the Classical Age and fifth century BC history, both Roman and Greek. She also owned and collected fine Etruscan vases. The

Etruscans were an ancient people who greatly influenced the Romans, though the Romans began suppressing them around 200 AD. To Peggy, Etruria represented mystery, intelligence, the beginning of our Western way of life, matrilineal inheritances and matrilineal clan systems, and a type of magical unknown world much like the revered Troy. Peggy later said that she wrote the *Etruscan Concerto* for the brilliant Florentine pianist Carlo Bussotti, whom she was keen to work with. She often wrote a work for a particular artist in the hope of working with them, and usually she was successful in her aim.

Bussotti, with Carlos Surinach as conductor, performed in the world premiere of the *Etruscan Concerto* at the Metropolitan Museum of Modern Art in New York in 1956. And a recording was made within a week of the first performance. On the cover of the MGM recording the music was described:

> The three movements of this highly coloured work present evocations of the moods of the Etruscan tombs of Tarquinia and [has] quotations from D. H. Lawrence's "Etruscan Places". One quote of his, taken from a piece entitled "Promenade" was: "You cannot think of art, but only of life itself, as if this were the very life of the Etruscans dancing in their coloured wraps with massive yet exuberant limbs, ruddy from the air, and the sea light, dancing and fluting along through the olive trees out in the fresh day".

The *Etruscan Concerto* was scored for piano and chamber orchestra and, like many of her previous works, was included in almost all the current music programs. Its mood was evocative of antiques, of sandy deserts, of nineteenth-century paintings. It was both evocative of the old and suggestive of all that is exotic in the new. A reviewer described the piece with reverence, 'Perhaps no other composer has known better how to express life through music to be used for dance than Peggy Glanville-Hicks. [This] latest work has the vitality and spirit of music which portrays life, its humour and pleasingly uncontrollable freedom.'[11]

By the mid- to late-fifties it sometimes seemed that P. G.-H. just couldn't miss. She even wrote incidental music for films, including commissioned projects, one for UNICEF carrying the title *A Scary Time*, and another for the United Nations, titled *The African Story*. She also scored music for cartoon and film graphics for various independent film makers.

Yehudi Menuhin was in New York giving concerts. During Peggy's earlier stay with him in California they had discussed the likelihood of an Indian music concert at the Museum of Modern Art, much in the vein of the earlier concerts like the Spanish concerts and the Music-for-Percussion concerts. With Peggy's status as Director of the Composers' Forum and occasional reviewer on the *New York Herald-Tribune*, the event was quickly set in motion with Peggy and Yehudi as co-hosts. It became yet another successful endeavour.

Peggy gave dinner parties at home for her friends, many of whom were fully active and employed in the music world. The slow starts and lost opportunities of the postwar period were long gone. Everyone seemed at the top of their careers. Most of Peggy's colleagues were now in their late forties. It was reasonably effortless for Peggy to secure financial backing for her projects and concerts. She used her privileged position to bring forward more young composers—'the untried and untested' as she called them. The Composers' Forum also continued to find and launch new talent. Peggy, like many of her peers, liked the opportunity of giving back.

Present at one of the parties she held in her Greenwich Village apartment were Yehudi Menuhin, her brother Beric from Melbourne, and Joaquín Nin-Culmell, brother of Anaïs Nin. Peggy considered Joaquín a composer-in-the-making. The party developed into a musical session and, according to Peggy's brother Beric, the music was astonishingly good. Joaquín and Peggy argued points of view and although he was younger than Peggy, he was not the baby composer she imagined. In fact Joaquín felt trapped by Peggy's image of him since he already enjoyed a considerable amount of success.

He never made his annoyance known to her but the friendship dwindled.

Oliver Daniels attended another soiree Peggy gave around this time. Daniels was the co-ordinating manager and editor of the American Composers' Alliance and later became the head of Broadcast Music Incorporated. He was to prove a lasting ally to Peggy in the recording industry. In America in 1989 he spoke to me about this particular party. He had arrived with Henry Cowell, then president of the American Composers' Alliance. Colin McPhee was engaged in a conversation with Peggy about gamelan music, the source of the rhythmic and melodic patterns that were later to dominate his compositions. McPhee had recently visited Bali where he had been greatly influenced (and where he eventually decided to reside permanently).

Peggy was extremely fond of McPhee and became impatient with Henry Cowell who tried to prise the two apart and inject himself into the conversation. Peggy began to attack Cowell and an argument ensued. Oliver diplomatically tried to quieten things down, but Peggy wanted to evict Cowell from the party. Her dismissive manner and strong opinions had resulted in her throwing guests out on other occasions. This time Cowell was spared, though at a previous party of Peggy's a racist remark concerning the composer Ulysses Kay had resulted in the young man in question being thrust out into the street. Had she been born male, physical violence might not have been beyond her; as it was, words and banishment of undesirables proved sufficient. Her acerbic tongue was feared by both readers and friends.

At the time of these parties, Oliver Daniels was engaged in producing music at CBS Television. CBS had a Sunday music program as well as performances by the New York Philharmonic Orchestra. During one season CBS put on their own symphony. They also had a late night show called 'Invitation to Music'. Because of these programs, which were produced by Daniels, he became well known in the contemporary music scene.

In later years Daniels wrote a monumental biography of conductor Leopold Stokowski. He introduced Stoki, as he was affectionately known, to Peggy at one of her parties. She had briefly encountered the famous Stoki only once before, he being the conductor, in her student days at the Royal College of Music, when she had secretly played the drummer in an ensemble class. Peggy's friendship with Stoki became something of a sparring match. There were many charged moments and differences of opinion between them. Peggy's imperious remarks were noted by Stoki.

Less visible in these and other gatherings were non-musical people and in particular female friends. Two women who were present at most of these gatherings were Katrina Castles and Silvia Spencer. Spencer was something of a semi-professional fundraiser, who was instrumental in persuading organisations to contribute to concerts. Daniels described her as 'a riot to talk to, batty as a fruitcake'. None the less there was a quiet respect for her gifts. Katrina Castles was described by Daniels as a flunky who seemed to accept being ordered around by Peggy. Castles was Australian and had studied to be a singer. Her role was that of helper, and she could always be relied upon to visit the sick or depressed of the musical coterie. Castles would compile lists of people interested in contemporary music for Peggy whenever an event was happening, and announcements would be sent out. During the fifties she spent much of her time with Peggy but it appeared an unequal relationship to outsiders.

Almost all of Peggy's friends and colleagues were male and homosexual. Peggy seemed to seek out homosexual men as friends, or it could be that there were more gay men working in music. It is difficult to know whether or not she acquired less positive opinions of women through her association with an all-male group. She may have needed male approval, though this is unlikely as she was known to always speak her mind whether she offended or not.

Peggy's husband had been homosexual, her lover rumoured to be bisexual. Her liberal views in matters of sexual preference were known: 'It is nobody's business.' When Paul Bowles held a social event and invited his regular crowd it was author Jane Bowles who was said to have been nasty to the men present, apparently because of their homosexuality. Oliver remembers her 'tearing through the house making offensive and confrontational remarks. She would sometimes ask everyone to leave if she was in a bad mood'. He was surprised at her apparent homophobia because Jane herself was lesbian.

It seems unlikely that Peggy had many opportunities for romantic encounters from within her own circle. This led many of her peers to believe she herself was either homosexual or asexual. Her discretion was impeccable. No information confirming either of these views was forthcoming and her emotional life remained relatively private. What is known is that after Paul Bowles, she had no significant relationships.

There were other women composers present in New York during Peggy's heyday and some were recording their work. The names of minor female composers occasionally appeared on recordings shared by Peggy; socially, however, the paths of Peggy and these women crossed rarely if ever. All-female programs were not common, but when they did occur the Glanville-Hicks name was there along with Elisabeth Lutyens.

In Minnesota, when Peggy was giving a series of lectures on contemporary music, she appeared before an organisation known as The Women's City Club. This club was completely run and organised by women and produced a journal. At the top of the front page of one issue of *Women's City Club News* was the statement: 'Women's City Club has no political, economic or social platform.' Underneath Peggy was billed to give a lecture entitled 'Music in our World', members and male guests allowed.

The *Evening Bulletin* in Philadelphia promoted a female composer concert series of chamber music, organised through the efforts of the Philadelphia Art Alliance. The list was impressive, including names such as Barbara Pentland from Canada, Grazyna Bacewicz from Poland, Louise Talma from New York and a posthumous piece by Lili Boulanger. Each of these composers enjoyed a distinguished career.[12]

Pentland had won a three year fellowship in composition at the Juilliard Graduate School in New York and had gone on to compose and teach theory and composition. Insufficient general interest in Canada and Canadian composers meant that much of her work, numbering some thirty scores at the time this concert was given, remained in manuscript form unpublished.

Louise Talma enjoyed much more attention and was Assistant Professor of Music at the Hunter College, New York. Achieving a masters in music and studying under Nadia Boulanger at the American Conservatory of Music in Fontainebleau in France, Talma carved quite a career for herself. She received many prizes and awards, the most notable being a Guggenheim Fellowship for two years in the late 1940s. Although Boulanger was reluctant to take on female private students at the time Peggy requested she school a number of women composers at the United States Conservatorium in France.

Grazyna Bacewicz graduated from Poland's Warsaw State Conservatory of Music and also studied composition with Nadia Boulanger. Bacewicz was approximately the same age as Peggy and although living in Warsaw was beginning to enjoy success abroad. She had already received a number of prizes in Paris prior to this concert series and had a list of symphonies, concertos and sonatas behind her.

Lili Boulanger has already been mentioned as the first woman to be awarded the Prix de Rome by the French Academy for composition. She was prevented by illness from participating in the musical activities of her time, but composed constantly, producing sufficient works by her death at age twenty-five to be considered an established composer. It was said at her death, 'Lili Boulanger passed like a meteor . . . the beauty she created will survive in the memory of her life and the quality of her work.'[13]

During the Philadelphia concerts Peggy felt for the first time that she was in the company of exceptional women and she commented, 'A lady composer (a term I have come to live with uneasily), as they would have it, has to be twice as good.' She knew that a female composer's road was not an easy one, that adequate composers of the female gender would never be tolerated or allowed to survive in the way that male composers were. On this topic she could be hostile, authoritarian or dismissive, depending on her audience, and yet she seemed to waver at times, denouncing gender differences as unimportant. She could be called a reluctant feminist.

The first long-playing record appeared towards the end of the forties and Peggy was intent on getting her music produced. Her Sonata for Harp, played by Zabeleta, was among the first to be recorded.

With each new production she aimed for the immortality of recordings. Oliver Daniels assisted her in gaining a recording of *The Transposed Heads* with Columbia Records. The record, according to Daniels, had barely enough space to accommodate the piece without cuts. Peggy refused to cut anything and a second disc had to be made. Despite rages and arguments and cajoling by Daniels, Peggy remained unaffected and the two records were made and distributed. During this time many recordings were lost as technology improved. Some resurfaced, to be re-recorded in the newer formats, others were lost forever. Later recordings of Peggy's work gave her the lasting form of promotion that ultimately assured her a place in musical history.

From 1932 to 1945 Peggy produced a sizeable list of works including an opera, three ballets, concerti for flute and for piano, a sinfonia, a cantata and numerous chamber pieces. But it was in the ten years that followed (1945–1955) that recordings made her music more visible.

The Concertino da Camera was recorded by Columbia Records, as was *Thomsoniana*; the Harp Sonata was recorded by Esoteric, the Sonata for Piano and Percussion by Columbia again along with several volumes of songs which had kicked off this productive period. *Letters from Morocco* premiered by Stokowski at the Museum of Modern Art, and the *Three Gymnopedie* was recorded by Remington. The *Sinfonia da Pacifica* was recorded by the Vienna Philharmonic for Composers' Recordings. Reviews ensured the ongoing success of her recorded works. For example:

> Peggy Glanville-Hicks composes music that is different. Some might call it 'modern' because it might not be what they are used to. It is music surprisingly easy to understand once her basic principles or ideas are grasped. She simply emphasises rhythm and melody over harmony. [She] develops two contrasting themes simultaneously rather than successively. Or she fuses melody and rhythm.[14]

Another review spoke of 'Miss Hick's gift for melody. It is enough to set her apart from many of her colleagues.'[15] Another commented: 'Here is music that is, to my ear, among the best of the new. Miss Glanville—Hicks is known for her highly individual, experimental music.'[16] A review by a woman jounalist from the *Buffalo Evening News* called Nell Lawson was particularly flattering. Lawson, who was unknown to Peggy, popped up at different times throughout her career with words of praise. She wrote of *Sinfonia Pacifica*:

> Peggy Glanville-Hicks holds a unique place in music for she is a top ranking composer in an art in which many women excel as executants, but few enter the list of the great composers. This young woman composer writes 'modern music' at its best.[17]

A glossy write-up on the back cover of a series by MGM Recordings called 'The American Composers' Series' was most unexpected. The *Gymnopedie* songs appeared with the works of Henry Brant and Dane Rudhyar and on the cover 'Miss Glanville-Hicks' was described as having 'an impressive output of works for orchestra, chamber groups, chamber vocal groups and films, which have been performed the world over, and have met with striking success.' George Antheil wrote on this same cover: 'A whole new world, aesthetically and expressively, has been revealed to me personally in her music, and I have no doubt that when it is opened up to others upon the scale that it deserves, they will agree with me; for the musical world of Peggy Glanville-Hicks is a very enthralling world, and it behoves us to listen with new ears.' Peggy's hard work was finally reaping its reward.

In 1957 MGM released a recording of *Concerto Romantico* using the MGM Orchestra. The violist was Walter Trampler for whom she had originally written the score, the conductor Carlos Surinach. The arrival of this work created something of a stir in avant-garde circles amongst colleagues and modern music fanciers. Peggy described herself as being 'in the dog house as a traitor to the cause'. On the record cover-notes of the MGM label she explained: 'The sudden re-inclusion of harmony and a non-dissonant harmony at that—plus the title "Romantico" seem to have been interpreted as a wanton and irresponsible return to the nineteenth century, and accusations of radical conservatism have been levelled at me from all directions.'

She went on to give her reasons for the departure from her usual musical idiom. She said that although she had always been an enemy of dissonance, it was a necessary change for her. It was not, she said, mere boredom but rather a distrust of composition systems, precipitated in recent years by her re-examination of music's primary impulses and units. A conviction had grown in her that melody and rhythm remained as the basic, perennial expressive and structural factors. In harmony, she said, the vertical concept reaches the end of the line. She had once thrown out harmony and with it dissonance. Structurally, she said, 'there was a gap left. Western large-scale forms evolved around diatonic harmony, as did also our orchestral layout.' On a more practical level she explained that percussive orchestration of busy themes would engulf the viola; and she also desired that the work be produced in a piano version.[18]

The 1957 edition of the *American Composers' Alliance*

Bulletin celebrated Peggy's recordings.[19] It quoted from a variety of publications which were reviewing her work. In the contemporary music scene this was quite an achievement.

Many of the recordings of Peggy's work occurred outside America and it was quite typical of Peggy to fly to Europe and supervise the production, invited or uninvited. This involved trips to Copenhagen, Paris, London and the like. Usually she doubled up and used the time in each country to negotiate further contracts, concert appearances or talks. She would tailor it, where possible, to have recordings take place near festivals in a specific region, capitalising on the quality of time spent.

She was chosen among a multitude of qualified musical experts in America to supply an American *Who's Who* for the famous Grove's *Dictionary*, a remarkable tribute to her talent and knowledge. This resulted in her compiling a listing of some 900 entries. It also justified many trips to Europe in the years that followed. During one such trip Peggy organised a supervisory recording detour to Denmark, and offered to give a lecture at the Danish International Musical Festival.[20] Her topic was 'Women Composers' and she managed to incorporate Australian composer Margaret Sutherland, giving a healthy impression of Australia and making herself seem less isolated. She denounced several eminent male critics for reviewing women composers as unintelligent, and elaborated on the difficulty of women composers working in slow-developing countries such as Australia, India and within Asia. On this occasion she spoke in French, a skill she had picked up while studying in Paris with Boulanger. Her audience seemed perplexed by the mention of women composers in faraway countries. Peggy told friends that this was one of the most satisfying lectures she had given.

On another mission to guard the safe passage of a recording she stopped off to give a lecture on the famous singer Maria Callas. In this lecture Peggy was searching for the qualities that set Callas apart: beauty of voice, stage presence, acting ability and so on. 'The magic of Callas is greater than the sum of its parts,' she said. 'The power of the fusion; fusion of ends and means, of the Dionysian expressive content, with the Apollonian formal proportion, that is the essence of things Greek. Greekness, underlying her individual magnitude as an artist has wrought this miracle.'

Peggy perceived in Callas a balance between intellectuality and sentimentality, essential and indicative of greatness in an artist. She described Callas as 'the born artist'.

In a time of specialisation and type-casting Callas remains adaptable. She does not hesitate to offer vocal sounds considered by tradition unbeautiful, even downright ugly! Such versatility [comes] from the deep centre where the end and its means are conceived as one, and from whence the concept has been brought into focus, muscle moves with mind toward the new expression.

She applauded the switch Callas could make from dramatic soprano to the mezzo range. From a discussion she had with Yehudi Menuhin, Peggy likened Callas to the changing from violin to viola. Menuhin had said to Peggy, 'It is not the weeks of practise, stretching the hand span to the larger instrument . . . but . . . time for the mind to absorb the moods of the new tone, the darker colours, and to speak in their language.'[21]

Next Peggy turned her assessment to Callas's recordings, in what she described as 'trying to distil the magic'. She began with Callas in Puccini's *Butterfly*. 'Most singers would meet the melodic opportunity with an outpouring, not Callas. She recognises the saturation of equally continuous sound. She holds a reserve, always, casting her vocal timbres from each section or aria. Callas,' she continued 'notes the dramatisation through tonal nuance, she has erratic pacing, a regard for the changing emotions.'

Peggy's lecture also described Callas's appearance in the production of Cherubini's *Medea* as the most sensational of all her performances, and also the beginning of her famous career.

'The difficulty of this piece,' said Peggy, 'is that it has an almost double tessitura—the voice lying consistently high in certain areas, dramatically low in others, with great leaps in between.'

Callas's acting ability did not escape scrutiny:

> In acting she has an ease in manner and stage movement, that she is mistress of the extremes in utter stillness or sudden violence, all are within her vocabulary. Alexis Minotis who directed her in the Epidauros productions, is talented, but it is Callas' type of stage action that is so persistently and peculiarly her own. The source of her originality and power is herself.

So moved was Peggy that she seemed unembarrassed by sentiment. At the lecture's end she said:

> In listening to Maria Callas one feels an impulse to arrest time, to stay the passing of so lovely a thing as though it could never again be recovered. It cannot, for music once over goes out and away—we know not where . . . Yet the miracle lies not in the thing created, but in the creator. A mystery momentarily revealed by an oracle who sits at its heart.[22]

Peggy had become so secure as a critic and composer that she knew she could make any type of public statement she wanted. Her recordings were assured. She said that the long playing microgroove record, designed for reproduction on turntables at thirty-three and a third revolutions per minute, spelt survival. She began casting around looking for new directions. Ballet had always intrigued her, there were musical possibilities still unexplored in dance. The shapes of the sounds could be different if the body was to give the music existence.

At night she would sit by her apartment window gloating over large colourful picture books about famous ballets that she had borrowed from the library. Ballet was so silent and beautiful. She pored over the books, some of them too large to find a space for. Strange new ballet sounds came from the gramophone on the shelf above the bed. The light overhead was a creamy white. She filled her small silver pipe with tobacco, little crusts of bark fell onto the books underneath. She smiled smugly and flashed a match to the pipe. She had set herself a new challenge.

NOTES

1. J. S. Harrison, *New York Times*, May 1952.
2. C.S., *New York Times*, May 1952.
3. J. S. Harrison, *New York Herald-Tribune*, 20 Aug. 1950.
4. *Colorado Springs Gazette*, 5 Aug. 1950.
5. Virgil Thomson, *New York Herald-Tribune*, 27 Aug. 1950.
6. George Antheil, *American Composers' Alliance Bulletin*, Vol. IV, No. 1, 1954.
7. 'This I Believe', New York radio series, 8 June 1954.
8. *Christian Science Monitor*, 10 April 1956.
9. Nell Lawson, *Buffalo Evening News*, 8 October 1956.
10. *Musical Times*, No. 95, 1954.
11. Anthony Cresswell, *Oregon Journal*, 2 Sept. 1954.
12. *Evening Bulletin*, Philadelphia, 21 April 1949.
13. Peggy Glanville-Hicks clipping. Undated. State Library of Victoria.
14. *Christian Science Monitor*, Oregon Journal, 2 Sept. 1956.
15. Gunby Rule, *Knoxville New Sentinel*, May 1956.
16. *Navy Times*, 5 Aug. 1956.
17. Nell Lawson, *Buffalo Evening News*, Oct. 1956.
18. MGM record cover (Peggy Glanville-Hicks: Concerto Romantico, Maga Richter: Aria and Toccata, Ben Weber: Rhapsodie Concertante).
19. *American Composers' Alliance Bulletin*, Vol. 6, No. 3, 1957.
20. London *Times*, unable to date (held in State Library of Victoria).
21. Peggy's lecture notes, State Library of Victoria.
22. Peggy's lecture notes, State Library of Victoria.

THE INTRIGUE
OF BALLET

By the late 1950s successful lectures, operatic compositions and musical commentary had made Peggy a name in America. Now the challenge of ballet possessed her. She began by writing short pieces of music for movement and as she explored this new form she would often screw up page after page of work. She would practise walking the length of her bed, as there was very little space to walk in her small apartment. When the right note clicked she would jump down onto the floor and quickly write it down before the idea evaporated. She would sing the bars and move her limbs robotically, puzzling over a distant unseizable musical concept. Ballet demanded something new of her. She longed to find a connection between music and movement, and she returned again to percussion instruments, music that compelled the body to move.

She talked to choreographer John Butler, and in the course of their discussions he asked her to write a score. Butler had been trained as a choreographer by the famous Martha Graham, whom Peggy knew from Greenwich Village. She had great faith in Butler, who had quite a reputation in New York, and she considered it an auspicious beginning. Peggy had contacted Butler once before during pre-production of *The Transposed Heads*. She had hoped to entice him to direct, but he was already engaged in another production. From the moment John Butler and Peggy met, a major friendship was born and the names of Butler and Glanville-Hicks were to occur together on numerous playbills. 'She's been driving me crazy ever since,' Butler later said.

The first in a line of ballet commissions Peggy received was from the Harkness Ballet Company. Butler had been asked to choose a composer and decided on Peggy. Together they produced *Masque of the Wild Man*.

I interviewed John Butler in New York in 1989 while Peggy was still alive. A man of great energy, but fearful of being trapped in the past, his views rushed out in disjointed sentences:

> I try to leave the composer free to be creative, to find the limitations within the skeleton. It's a large question mark on both sides when the composer and director–choreographer are commissioned but I love it. Who knows what will turn out? One is usually limited to existing music. Commissions are much more exciting.

Turning to the topic of Peggy: 'Peggy is bossy as a friend, but never in the work situation. She would never transgress on another artist's ground, but socially she was a little bitch.'

Butler hunted through his memory for images to reconstruct her.

> She never wasted time . . . She was not polite, she either liked you or she didn't . . . I was aware of her reputation on the *New York Herald-Tribune* and she was often quoted, long after an article appeared, sometimes years afterwards . . . She was very opinionated, always dominating. I didn't fall out with her as others did. I was one of the few people in the world that she was scared of. She would let me have it but eventually I would top her. Some of my friends said 'Why in the hell do you put up with that bitch? What are you doing?' She could be so unpleasant but then they all admit that she's fascinating, she's worth it, she always made an effort intellectually to be with people.
>
> (John) Cage and she were extremely close, and socially I was in fact on the other side because Cage had a friend Les (Merce) Cunningham whose place I took up as a little dancer when I first came to New York. Cage and Cunningham would scoff and laugh at the public, but they both did very interesting work. Then there was Sandra Levie and Paul Bowles and

they all were involved somehow. Peggy got very involved with Paul Bowles. I was green compared to them and sometimes I felt like the enemy around that group. Peggy never made me feel like that, she was an equal with me but not necessarily with anyone else. She lived in a type of ivory tower and could be very snobby about people. She liked me and Virgil [Thomson] and so and so, always names that she could toss about. She always rode with the best and then became one! I loved her, even though she would outrage me, but then I could still knock her down.

Peggy's friendship with Butler continued for years, becoming more brother–sister like than either would have expected. Peggy once said of him, 'Giovanni [her pet name for him]— I never thought we'd get on. He could be so precocious and so pushy but I adored him. He was a poppet and what a talented choreographer, the best.' For thirty years Butler and Peggy exchanged postcards.

Butler enjoyed her intellect. They would discuss issues such as 'technique and inspiration' at a depth others failed to grapple with. Peggy published papers on many of the issues they discussed for publications such as the *Juilliard Review*. She liked to write on topics of controversy like the hybridisation of jazz and contemporary music, or opera in America. Butler was excited by the possibilities of change. Peggy dared to write of it.

Peggy liked to explain in her articles the complexities of composition. In response to a journalist who described the art of composition as non-intellectual, she penned the following response:

> It has been said of the composer that her materials lie in the territory of the physicist, her technique in the territory of the mathematician and her message in the category of the prophet . . . Certainly the composer's span of awareness embraces two areas; the merged level of the intellect wherein is cultivated the technical skill and mastery, and another submerged level from whence springs her inspiration, and

where an instinctive rather than calculated choice appears to reign. The whole is like an iceberg, whose submerged mass provides the stability supporting the emerged peaks. From the buried mass comes the eternal potency, while above the surface, like a long line of ancestors, are the forms and idiomatic patterns in all their geographic and historic variety in which this expressive volume incarnates. It is a duality of the spirit and body; and the quality of greatness in art has a lot to do with the degree of poise and balance with which these two halves relate to each other and act together.[1]

Peggy wrote positively about the freshness of rhythm she found in composers who chose to cross-pollinate jazz with the musical academy techniques. She said of them:

This movement is going on with all the vigor and vitality of the crossbreed . . . (Henry) Brant's racy score [marries jazz clichés, specifically those of the early forties] and is terrific fun! . . . Jazz is rich in the subconscious factor . . . A mad and wonderful contribution to the music melting pot of America.[2]

This was an unpopular discussion. Jazz idioms in concert halls and instrumental ensembles were frowned upon, especially in highbrow circles. Peggy herself never wrote jazz but she admired innovation.

In an *American Composers' Alliance Bulletin* article she discussed opera and the absence of home-grown American opera. She openly criticised large venues such as the City Centre for failing to introduce American audiences to opera. At the same time she argued against over-reacting by excluding European operas. 'A nationalistic approach . . . misses the mark. It is every bit as galling to the one or two real born operatic composers on the local scene to see a unique opportunity handed to, say, Copland—whose gift is great, but not for opera.'

Butler would rub his hands together with glee, as no doubt many others did, when P.G.-H. ripped into the establishment and Copland, although criticised by her, was a personal friend.

Peggy's quest to find an appropriate musical form for ballet had become a preoccupation. In the evenings at home she would labour over *Masque of the Wild Man*. The Harkness Ballet company wanted the work ready in time for the Spoleto Festival of 1958. John Butler was also priming her for a second ballet commissioned from CBS TV the following year, called *Saul and the Witch of Endor*.

Peggy looked over her earlier ballet scores which were: *Caedmon*, *Hylas and the Nymphs*, *Postman's Knock*; and *Dance Cantata for Soloists*, which had been part of a recent experimentation. These works achieved only amateur status and Peggy did not regard them as significant in any way. Perhaps no choreographer took an interest in them. Perhaps Peggy did not wish to have them taken seriously. *Postman's Knock* had an American production, but it was on a small scale, with student dancers. None of these works gave her the drive or motivation that she felt for *Masque of the Wild Man*. It was as if these earlier ballets, modest though they were, had failed to inspire her. She was determined to begin again. So while the rest of her career absorbed her days, at night she began searching for the unknown musical quality that approximated movement. She visited the library in the evenings and brought home endless books, hoping to trigger something in herself that would transform her music in some miraculous way.

Peggy's other scores, outside of dance, were by now finding their way to remote corners of the world. In 1959[3] the *Palestine Post* reviewed a mini-retrospective presentation of some of her music which was included in a concert by the International Society of Music in Tel Aviv. Work by Elisabeth Lutyens, along with an Israeli composer, H. Neugarten, and American composer David Diamond was played in the same program. Described as an admirable performance, this event and many others like it made Peggy realise that her work had a life of its own and she would not always be there to supervise its birth and introduction.

She had made a lot of important friends during these days of success and musical enterprise. She was no longer the young ambitious composer hoping to attend the right parties and make connections; rather she was the popular P.G.-H., on every guest list that mattered. She was not by nature a socialite in the negative sense, but she did have a penchant for artistic talent and preferred like-minded friends. By the end of the fifties, production organisers were courting her. She no longer had to invent the program or idea in which her music could be played. Producers came to her.

Earlier there had been occasions when she ghost-wrote music for other composers who were unable to complete a commission in time for a particular production. Peggy as a young unknown had grabbed the opportunity for the money. She had even felt a certain pride in being able to fulfil the commercial requirements, completing a score in just a few days, sometimes staying up all night to do so. But by 1955, short of helping a friend out, Peggy no longer took up the slack for film, ballet, television or theatre companies who had hired themselves an incompetent composer in the first place. Now she demanded commissions and got them. It was an insult to ask her to fill in and rectify the botched job of someone else.

Looking back at her early unrecognised work, Peggy said: 'In the big city of New York risks are taken every minute as they should be. What is despicable is that the new artist is not given the credit she or he deserves.' Her feelings of gratitude were mixed. She had a history of work that would remain hidden under the names of male composers she had never met. Her cleverness in being able to complete an unfinished score in record time was only relevant to those involved. As far as the wider world of music was concerned she had produced only that which appeared under the initials P.G.-H.

Towards the end of the fifties, relaxed, and with a career established, Peggy began to allow her work to be played at select venues and the salons of the wealthy. A concert sponsored by the Library of Congress under the auspices of the Elizabeth Sprague Coolidge Foundation was held in the Coolidge Auditorium in January, 1958. The best-known names in literature, film and music turned out for the event. Autographed manuscripts were on display in the foyer, and the corridor leading to the auditorium displayed pictures of famous composers throughout history. Signed scores were housed under glass. This concert was broadcast in its entirety by radio station WGMS of Washington, DC, and made available to affiliated stations of the Good Music Network. The program read:

1. Luigi Boccherini (1743–1805) String Quartet in D major, Op. 24, No. 5 (1778)
2. Wolfgang Amadeus Mozart (1756–1791) String Quartet in G major, K.V.387 (1782)
3. Peggy Glanville-Hicks (b. 1912) Concertino Antico, for harp and string quartet (1955)
4. Ludwig van Beethoven (1770–1827) String Quartet in E minor, Op. 59, No. 2 (1806)

It is obvious from the program that living composers had a long wait ahead of them before they could fill a program without the greats of history breathing down their necks. Music, and in particular classical music, as the lay person distinguishes it, is conservative. Music was respectable and people such as her friend John Cage were not overly encouraged by the musical establishment. In fact Cage and others like him were castigated for mocking music and for daring to tease their respectable audiences. Their sin was to experiment with the medium.

With the exception of her tendency to incorporate folkish elements into the work, Peggy did not qualify as radical. She was known to have a liking structurally for Eastern, particularly Indian, music. She spoke highly of percussion instruments and dared to incorporate some of these ideas into her work. Fortunately for her reputation, this tendency was expressed with the greatest subtlety and her more conservative audiences forgave her.

At some level it was expected that a woman composer's work would be romantic, feminine and sweet. Peggy enjoyed the rowdiness and gutsiness of opera. She preferred the loud voices of men rather than the angel pitch of women. She had a personal dislike of the squeaky notes given to women sopranos and experimented a little, giving women deeper notes to sing. It was her view that women in opera should not always be 'the shattering element'.

It was a great source of vexation to friends that Peggy believed she had a monopoly on good taste. Yet Peggy's certainty and independent views also endeared her to her friends. She was usually straightforward, direct and spontaneous, and if this was her least liked side, it was also her most admired quality, for it indicated that she had clear goals and took on challenges. She was distinguished not only by her dress or her Australian–English accent but by her enthusiasm for all things new and untried. She encouraged others to take risks. She assisted people in obtaining painting or sculpture exhibitions. She made opportunities for young composers. She put clothing designers in touch with celebrities, provided journalists with subjects for articles, promoters with those who needed publicity and sponsors with needy and talented artists. She herself had little money.

When success comes in the arts, money does not automatically follow. For many artists well-paying jobs are intermittent. The creator does not fare nearly as well as salaried promoters. It was this fact that first prompted Peggy to consider buying a home outside America. In Manhattan she could only afford a small one bedroom apartment which she would have to spend her entire life paying for. Some of her artistic friends had bought villas in Italy or Greece. Peggy became interested in this option and decided to join some of them on their holidays. It would be a new experience to travel abroad with a view to setting up a home and she approached it with an open mind.

The first such trip she took was with Jac Murphy. Jac was in press and publicity and was well known in the arts for his management skills and organisation of national tours. In New York in 1989, he filled me in on the history of his acquaintance with Peggy. He had just left the Marine Corps when he met Peggy, having completed his training in Australia, and was dividing his time between Florence and New York. He was heavily engaged in management of touring orchestras and small chamber orchestras. 'After the war,' Jac said, 'many writers, artists and composers stayed on in Europe. Some of us bought houses and tried to find work.' He explained that most artists first explored where their particular art might be advanced and appreciated; and then planned 'how to get there and get things happening'. He and Peggy were both great organisers, as Jac saw it. He described Peggy and himself as 'useful names'. 'Names were invited to festivals and dinner parties,' he said. He spoke of Peggy with admiration: 'Peggy was thought of as an aristocrat, an opinion of her that came not out of any loyalty to England or the royal family but out of her authoritarian tongue.' He was referring to how her opinions somehow became law and few dared to contradict her. He had a curious way of praising Peggy. 'She is a very good critic, excellent grammar and she knows music, ah huh!'

Jac didn't recall Peggy discussing her own music but found her harsh in her judgements of others. He was shocked that she dared to criticise the distinguished American composer Sam Barber. Jac quickly learned that the opinionated P.G.-H. could dismiss Beethoven and a contemporary in the same breath without regret or apology. For Peggy, music knew no time, no century, there was only good music or none at all and she was the best judge. Being an official critic only legitimised her opinions. 'She was paid to give opinion,' Jac said. It wasn't that the position had gone to her head, rather she was a natural critic. She had thought about little other than music all her life.

Peggy and Jac had long discussions about techniques for

promoting music, tour management, and publicity gags. Jac could teach Peggy a great deal, and as director of various music committees she listened eagerly. She was always at work trying to launch some new musical project. She admired the type of energy professionals like Jac had.

The summer before Jac and Peggy visited Florence, he rented his house out to Thomas Mann's daughter. When Peggy arrived she was pleased to see that Elizabeth Mann, the same girl whom Paul Bowles had seen with Jane Auer in the taxi, had become so entranced with the place that she took up permanent residence next door. During this visit several friends arrived in town, including Oliver Daniels, Noel Jenkins and Carlo Bussotti. Peggy had written a work for each of them at various times, and they often called in to chat. Jac was managing an Italian production of 'Piccola Accademia Musicale' at the time, so Peggy entertained her friends. When Thomas Mann and his family arrived to stay next door, the entire household was invited into Jac's house for afternoon tea. On this occasion it developed into a musical soiree and extended into the early hours of the morning.

Carlo Bussotti was the most frequent visitor and he and Peggy went to concerts together. They came home late in the evenings full of talk about modern music and ballet. They attended various local performances, including opera. Bussotti was involved in everything 'modern' and had played piano for a Columbia recording of Peggy's Sonata for Piano and Percussion as well as the piece Concertino da Camera.

In addition to social outings, Peggy used the daytime in Florence to concentrate on the scores for *Masque of the Wild Man* and *Saul and the Witch of Endor*. She did not find the time to seriously look at the real estate market as she had intended.

This particular trip was to have special significance because Peggy and Paul Bowles had planned to meet up for a brief holiday. Jac said: 'Near Bowles' arrival date Peggy became increasingly joyful.' As a favour to Jac for his kind hospitality and a measure of her generally euphoric spirits, she had written a piece on his musicale for the *New York Herald-Tribune*. Jac woke up one morning to find the review on the table and Peggy missing. He recalled that the previous night Bowles had arrived and was talking with the neighbours, and the next minute he and Peggy were gone. He imagined they had just taken an evening walk but realised later that Peggy must have left the review on the table as a parting gesture. 'Bowles certainly had the ability to bring out the most spontaneous of habits in Peggy,' said Jac. 'No doubt they made for a cottage somewhere by the seaside.'

Peggy visited Jac in Florence on a second occasion, with the conductor of the Louisville Kentucky Symphony, Moritz Bomhard, in tow. *The Transposed Heads* production was discussed with the Mann family next door. Thomas Mann had died before this second visit. Peggy recalled that Thomas Mann's wife was not happy with the opera and felt that the story she and Thomas Mann had put together was not true to his book. For these reasons Peggy broke all connections with the Mann family.

Jac seemed fascinated by the affair between Peggy and Bomhard at the time of the second visit. He remembered Bomhard as obsessed by Peggy. 'He was physically inseparable from her the entire time.' Bomhard was a presenter of modern music and it is likely that Peggy and Bussotti, on her previous visit to Jac's, attended performances given by him. 'She certainly had a knowledge of him before receiving her commission for *The Transposed Heads*,' said Jac, alluding to the possibility of favouritism.

Jac also recalled his visits to Peggy in New York. He described a small one-room apartment with a stove in the corner, where she loved to entertain. 'She would have people over for drinks but would rarely cook,' he said. Visitors had to sit on the bed, as there wasn't enough room for additional chairs. Jac most admired Peggy for her wit and sense of the incredible—her stories of an unexpected success or the eccentricity of a neighbour hanging out the washing in the rain. She loved the absurd. 'She had a high snicker of a laugh,' he said. She was also prone to falling out with friends, such as the conductor Noel Jenkins, or choreographer John Butler. (A later interview revealed that Butler, like Jac himself, always saw other men as the enemy, never themselves. Curiously, both denied ever falling out with her.)

Her New York life remained vibrant. Jac recalled Peggy's friend Mrs Courtney Campbell, who not only attended Peggy's drinks parties but accompanied Peggy to concerts. There were not many women close to Peggy, but Campbell, who was a poet, known to her friends as Peggy rather than Courtney, lived nearby on Tenth Street. Peggy Glanville-Hicks regarded Campbell as a competent poet. Campbell introduced her to poets and writers whom she found an immediate rapport with.

Jac also remembered the 'Virgil Thomson–John Cage crowd' attending drinks parties at Peggy's apartment. Virgil Thomson would reciprocate with dinners at his apartment in the Chelsa Hotel. His were the best events, according to Jac, partly because there was food served as well as drinks. Thomson's and Glanville-Hicks' gatherings were the envy of the uninvited.

Peggy, according to Jac, had become a celebrity. 'People wanted to talk to her all the time,' he said. 'Peggy was known to be difficult to impress, but if she took an interest in someone she needed to know everything.' Jac believed that sometimes she went too far in this and was too earnest in her discovery. He also described her as bossy and the type of person one felt obliged to answer. Jac felt it was this intense focus and curiosity that caused her relationships with men to be brief and dramatic. When the mystery unravelled, she lost interest.

Jac remembered a rare occasion, at the time of Stanley Bate's death, when Peggy confessed to him her feeling that Bate had ruined her life. When Stanley died their marriage details became public. There was talk of his financial recklessness and homosexual offences. Peggy felt pitied and she detested it. Somehow Stanley's death cast one last shadow over her. She worried that she would lose credibility as a strong, respectable, private individual. The marriage had not only been a failure, but a sham. The gossip and public commentary after his death made Peggy both depressed and defensive. She had married a talented composer and needed to remain proud of the fact. It was her view that an artist could be forgiven many things if the work contributed was worthy. She had loved Bate, yet somehow his death had made her look a fool. 'Stanley,' she said, 'had ended everything by his suicide.'

Despite the gossips and cynics, Peggy's music was being played, she had some wonderful friends and acquaintances, and her opinions were in print. She had achieved all she had hoped for and yet privately she felt harmed by the gossip. She began to question herself. She had several panic attacks, and began drinking too much at social events. She made jokes about the female midlife crisis to friends. Her enthusiasm for her work was even dampened at times. Fortunately the scores for the two ballets had been completed at Jac's in Florence. While the company moved into rehearsal stage, Peggy paused temporarily from work.

She should not have been feeling that 'something was missing'. Her work was continuing to turn up in the most likely and unlikely venues around the US. The *Philadelphia Inquirer* in 1958 reported on *Concertino Antico*, performed by the Juilliard String Quartet in Goodhart Hall, Bryn Mawr College. This commissioned piece welcomed Peggy back into the anti-dissonance school. The *New York Times* recorded her inclusion in a variety concert, entitled 'Music in Our Time'. The premiere piece was again *Concertino Antico* for harp and string quartet. It was described by the reviewer as having 'gap scales' and was well received. Peggy's friend Carlos Surinach arrived to conduct a work of hers at the Metropolitan Museum of Art. Leopold Stokowski also conducted her piece *Letters from Morocco* at an American Musical Festival around this time.[4]

The famous Town Hall on 123 West 43rd Street, New York, was host to the WNYC Annual American Music

Festival. WNYC and WNYC–FM were the municipal broadcasting systems for the city of New York. The concert Peggy was to be part of was only one of more than one hundred special programs scheduled for the festival. Peggy's work appeared on the program alongside that of composer David Diamond, her inclusion being *Drama For Orchestra*. Diamond's work was Concerto For Chamber Orchestra. Diamond was of similar age and had also studied with Nadia Boulanger. The two had first met in Paris. Diamond received numerous commissions and won many awards and scholarships in his career as a composer. Peggy and he met several times throughout her musical career but never really forged a bond. Diamond settled in Florence and visited her at Jac Murphy's house in Florence, but despite his respect for her work a lasting friendship did not ensue. Peggy considered him too moody, a bit of a wet blanket socially, and Diamond failed to hold her interest in conversation; but she remained respectful of his work.

By 1959, Peggy's work on the two ballets began to pay off. The ballet *Masque of the Wild Man*, with its blend of her score and Butler's choreography, was reportedly superb. The second commission from CBS Television for the ballet *Saul and the Witch of Endor* was also a success. This music written for trumpet, percussion and strings appeared as part of a program called 'Lamp Unto My Feet'. Peggy felt pleased with her efforts. She enjoyed the exposure that television could give, but it was not enough.

She had ideas for more ballets that she still needed to work on. At this time she also wrote some smaller scores for less significant ballets which were not reviewed. Ballets were generally not reviewed as often as other forms of music at this time, and those that were tended to concentrate on the talent of the choreographer and leading dancers rather than that of the composer.

Peggy felt only momentarily satisfied by the success of her ballet scores. She felt the work that she had long been experimenting with was falling into place. All that she lacked was a larger ballet work but for now this would have to wait. 'Timing was crucial', as Peggy liked to repeat.

In recognition of her creative work in music the American Institute of Arts and Letters awarded her $1,000, a tribute of high degree for the composer and music critic of twelve years' standing. Newspapers across the world reported this prestigious honour to 'one of the most knowledgeable music critics around town'.

Australian newspapers showed their pride. Australian audiences, however, had largely forgotten her and while select music circles knew something about Peggy, most did not. Expatriates have often paid an unduly high price for their apparent lack of loyalty.

Great changes were taking place musically in Australia by the beginning of the sixties. The first Adelaide Arts Festival took place in 1960. Richard Meale's Sonata for Flute and Piano was performed at the International Society for Contemporary Music festival in Amsterdam. In 1961 Igor Stravinsky visited to conduct performances of his own work. By 1963 a Sydney branch of the International Society had begun a program of public recitals. In 1964 the Tasmanian Conservatorium of Music was established and the Canberra School of Music formed. And in 1965 the Sydney Symphony Orchestra undertook its first extensive overseas trip. Peggy followed all of these developments in newspapers sent to her from Australia.

After recovering from the depression associated with Stanley's death she became plagued with sporadic illnesses. Mostly these were colds and coughs and of no major concern, but a new ailment had begun to disturb her. Her vision became periodically clouded and she suffered severe headaches. She attributed this menacing development to her previous emotional state, spoke of experiencing some type of midlife crisis and appeared less in public. She also began avoiding most social occasions. Her failing sight did not go unnoticed, and the whisper soon got out that Peggy was going blind. Frightened and unsure of herself, she did nothing to stem the rumours. At times her sight deteriorated to such a degree that she remained shut up in her apartment for a week at a time. The headaches also grew more frequent.

She decided that what she needed was a change of climate away from the stress of New York. Jac Murphy and she discussed her purchasing a house abroad. An inheritance from her mother's family estate finally came through, and with little hesitation she boarded a boat, not for Italy as Jac had expected, but for Greece.

Greece held special fascination for her as she had become increasingly involved in oriental music, searching for a new musical form to add dimension to her work. In her own words:

> The monophonic structure I had evolved already. I was looking for a melodic style which contained within itself quite definite rhythm. English folk music doesn't have it. I needed to integrate rhythm into a piece without always having to depend on the percussion department. Bartók had left archives which alluded to this thing I was looking for. I remember him saying at the ISCM—the further you go south the greater the rhythm gets! I continued to research. I looked at [Bartók's] scores and notes, offering a Mediterranean version of this. Next I began to collect Greek music and then the balloon went up, I knew I had found traces of what I was looking for, wonderful rhythms I found too. An organic melody rhythm. So I applied for a grant to travel to Greece for what I thought would be one year. I took with me a tape machine and recorded from everywhere, dance halls, dialogues, funny old instruments. I had struck solid gold. This was to form the basis for a later ballet, *Nausicaa*.

Her initial period of work in Greece was to be one of her most fruitful. She didn't know anyone there and couldn't speak a word of Greek and could therefore concentrate purely on her work: She said:

> I would start with a theme. I would be in a great state of tension until I could get the curtain down on a scene. Then I would go out on a bender and listen to some bouzouki

and eat steak in a tavern. At other times I would eat at one of those closed-in restaurants, anywhere that was cheap and quick. The work would come out whole as a monolith. It requires this but rarely does one work under the best of circumstances.

Peggy initially stayed in a cheap *pension*. At the end of her frenzied work period, she walked the ancient streets in search of a suitable house. New York had been rewarding artistically but financially life had been uncomfortable. Peggy was nearing fifty (as she said from forty-five onwards). She wanted a few home comforts as well as artistic challenges. The inheritance Peggy's mother had left her made up an annual allowance of £1,200. Peggy purchased her first house for just £3,000. This was security at last. She decorated it in the traditional local style and it became a quiet and comfortable refuge for her. Yet paradoxically, three months later when Peggy was fund-raising to produce a work of her own in Greece, one of the first things she considered selling was the house. It was ultimately spared, although she never took selling it off the list of possibilities.

Her health seemed to have improved. She began financial negotiations for the production of *Nausicaa*. Obsessed with the idea of entering the Athens Festival, she began writing letters. These long letters outlined her requirements for artistic crew, the planning and booking of production space, publicity costs, costumes and so on. She secured a place in the program; all that she needed then were the funds to pay everyone. She became desperate; her letters to funding authorities changed from polite notes of introduction to demanding tirades. In one particularly desperate letter she ended the piece with 'I do not have time to await decisions!' One irate but positive sponsor reacted to the stiff letters with: 'Dear Nausicaa, about the money, O.K. so stop now, my secretary has tired of writing to you.' But Peggy did not stop. By day she wrote letters and by night she wrote music. This was the challenge that she had been waiting for.

The role of producer was not a new one for Peggy but the stakes were high because of the short lead-up time. It was January 1961 and the festival was due to open in August. American sponsors were hesitant. The Athens Festival was considered a Greek event. The headaches she had previously been experiencing returned intermittently. A noticeable difference was her impatient behaviour, especially with financiers.

Peggy had always admired the writer Robert Graves. She was fascinated by his non-Christian views on the story of Christ and liked to quote from his work. Graves' interest in archaeology and anthropology sat comfortably with her own. She admired him for his mysterious approach to religion, despite her conventional Protestant upbringing. In the summer of 1956 Peggy spent several months on the island of Majorca working with Graves on the libretto for *Nausicaa*. As usual the ground work had taken longer than the creative process. She had spent a considerable time writing to his publishers seeking rights to write the libretto for *Nausicaa*, basing it on his novel *Homer's Daughter*.

After some lengthy letters and discussion with his publishers Graves himself wrote, inviting her to visit him in Majorca. Peggy set off on the rather complicated journey, first by boat and then by bus. She found a delightful little hotel in a town quite near Graves' house. After all the booking formalities, the baggage was stored and Peggy took a walk through the dusty streets in search of a crisp salad and a chilled glass of wine. She had not walked two blocks when who should turn the corner but Robert Graves! He looked exactly as Peggy imagined him, 'all wiry and sophisticated'. They halted in the street and looked at one another. 'Are you by any chance P.G.-H.?' he asked. 'Yes,' said Peggy, 'and you are Robert Graves?' Her stare was obvious and she imagined herself to be blushing. Graves also behaved slightly out of character by telling her, 'You can use anything

I've written in *any* way you like.' Peggy wasn't listening properly and forgot to ask him to put it in writing. Later that night in her hotel room she was cranky with herself for missing this professional detail. He was, however, true to his word and proved to be very co-operative in the writing of the libretto.[5]

Graves was a good deal older than Peggy and while it seems unlikely that anything romantic ever took place, it is likely that the flirtation was mutual. At the end of several months when Peggy emerged with the script of *Nausicaa* and an almost completed score, she made comments to John Butler which implied that she was more familiar and less enamoured with the genius writer than when they first met. 'Robert,' she told him, 'would say that he considered himself a poet who wrote a few novels from time to time to make some money. I don't think his poems are really that good but the novels are stupendous.' This irreverence might have been mere Glanville-Hicks humour.

Back in Greece, Peggy embarked on a part-time research program into Greek folk music. She spent many enjoyable months digging in the archives of the Academy of Athens for source materials. Of particular importance was her research into scales and metrics of demotic music. The final *Nausicaa* score drew on musical idioms from regions as diverse as Epirus, the Peloponnese, Crete and the Dodecanese.

Set in the 7th century BC at the Palace of Drepanum, a Greek city state in Western Sicily, the story of Nausicaa is similar to the adventures of Odysseus. The characters of Penelope and Nausicaa are merged into one, and Odysseus becomes Aethon, a shipwrecked Cretan nobleman. There is a challenge laid for Nausicaa's hand. Penelope, who claimed she would settle on a husband as soon as she finished knitting her garment, would every night unravel the knitting. Nausicaa does likewise. A secondary plot is woven around Robert Graves' idea that the *Odyssey* was not written by Homer but by a woman; the Princess Nausicaa reveals herself as the real author, and how and why she came to write it.

Time magazine summarised the story:

> Princess Nausicaa hears a group of young noblemen, her suitors, planning to overthrow her father, King Alcinous. She plots against the suitors, sees them all killed, and asks only one thing as her reward: 'I demand that in future it will be / My version of a faithful Penelope / My story of this palace war / My account of the part women played that you will sing.'[6]

The first artist to be engaged in the production of *Nausicaa* was John Butler. He was to direct and choreograph it. John decided to join Peggy in Greece to discuss casting. Peggy was keen to employ a Greek singer Teresa Stratas. The rest of the dancers, with the exception of a professional male lead, would all be local. The music was to be conducted by Carlos Surinach. He was reliable and talented and had conducted for Butler before.

John thought Peggy's decisions rash but couldn't resist her spontaneity. His methods of working were revealing. An extremely handsome man with delicate skin, he insisted on remaining in the air-conditioned comfort of his hotel room, where he invited Peggy to join him at work. One of John's outstanding features was his eyebrows and on the rare occasion when he visited Peggy at home, he would poke his head inside her door to surprise her. She would laugh riotously, exclaiming that his eyebrows had entered the room five minutes before he had. John always arrived complaining about the heat. Peggy protected him from both the weather and the gravity of the financial situation surrounding *Nausicaa*. The burden of production was entirely hers, and despite difficulties the cheques began to arrive, some a little later than desired.

Peggy agreed to let John rehearse from midnight to sunrise to avoid the intensity of the heat during the day. When the casting was complete, John and his dancers trekked up to the Herodes Atticus theatre every midnight after other concerts had closed. The night air was warm; the dancers, bathed in moonlight, flung themselves around the ancient stone theatre, the sound of their soft leather shoes scuffing the floor like a hair broom. Sometimes they would pretend to be the whimsical Isadora Duncan, at other times their cool limbs would chill and they would all stand erect like marble statues. When the first ray of light struck, there would be a theatrical scurry and the dancers would gleefully disappear. Some elements of the dance were fashioned after the figures that appeared on Greek pottery. Butler especially enjoyed the fusion of the gods and the dance.

Robert Graves arrived in Greece by plane. Peggy persuaded John Butler to venture out into the sun to collect Graves from the airport. Graves stepped onto the tarmac wearing one black shoe and one brown. He stared up into the Greek sky with joy then knelt on his knees and kissed the ground in dramatic papal fashion. For three days John and Peggy showed Robert the sights of Greece. Finally, on the third day, in exasperation Peggy turned to face him and said: 'Robert I can't stand it another minute. For three days you have said absolutely nothing. I know you have never travelled to Greece before. What do you think?' For all his writings on Greek mythology Graves had never been on Greek soil. His erudite descriptions were taken from things he had read and researched. From imagination only he had reconstructed a reality. After a pause Graves turned to John and Peggy and in a nonchalant fashion said, 'It's exactly as I remembered it!'

During the days that followed, Graves exhibited an uncanny knack of finding walking paths that had become invisible due to vegetation, or long forgotten sites, or missing segments of ancient pots, as if he was in familiar surroundings. On one occasion when he and Peggy were travelling to Delphi, Graves suddenly urged Peggy to stop the car and let him out. He exclaimed, 'There is something here, I feel it. I must see. I know.' They had stopped at an oracle site. Peggy and he ventured into a semi-excavated area when Graves looked at her sheepishly, 'Now I wonder where it was that Socrates used to sit. No, I think it was over here, Peggy.' He turned full circle and walked several paces sideways, 'Ah ha, there is the small stream that used to run under a shop where he would wet the leather.' Graves kicked around and turned up a few ancient pieces of metal which he claimed were the remnants of nails that Socrates had used while mending shoes. Peggy later made formal enquiries and discovered that Graves' reckoning had been absolutely correct.

Graves proved to be an asset with pre-publicity work. He would speak on radio promoting the work with his stories of intrigue. Peggy was a little dismayed when he appeared at the radio station without his teeth, so absent-minded was he about unimportant details; but something of his genius must have aroused the interest of listeners.

Nausicaa had finally taken shape. The choreography was complete; the conductor and musicians ready. Peggy felt she had found the musical nuances that her former work lacked. The music had a peculiar flavour of its own: part-Greek, part-Indian. Sometimes evocative of endless Greek skies and sea, at other times evoking a village scene in India with food cooking, and bangles clanging on the arms of women as they worked. Industrious at one moment, peaceful at another. The music revealed an ancient world of trickery and charm.

Nausicaa was exquisitely fashioned. The performers wore exotic Greek costumes with inlaid jewels. They moved inside an ancient stone cathedral, a world befitting Odysseus or Nausicaa. At the last dress rehearseal Peggy, Carlos Surinach and Robert Graves all sat together on a stone bench near the edge of the stage. The last dancer left the stage. There was no applauding, no audience except the production team. 'Well, what do you think?' John Butler had posed the inevitable question. Everyone was silent. The next evening a ten minute standing ovation greeted the world premiere of Peggy Glanville-Hicks' *Nausicaa*, in the ancient theatre of Herodes Atticus at the base of the Acropolis. The cast of 150 received eight curtain calls from the capacity crowd of 4,800. A second ten minute standing ovation greeted the composer and her artistic collaborators.

The 1961 Athens Festival opened with *Nausicaa* billed and reviewed as a 'phenomenal international work'.[7] The open-air theatre was packed beyond capacity with people queued and pushed as far back as the Parthenon. People crowded into the aisles and onto the base of the stage. Reviews were glowing and appeared in almost every country in the world. It was applauded in France for its unforgettable qualities, in Germany for its style and timelessness, in Greece for its astounding beauty, in England for its international qualities and in the US as an idiom unique of its kind.[8] Peggy had hit the biggest event of her life, larger and more grandiose than she had ever imagined. This was her pinnacle.

NOTES

1. *Juilliard Review*, edition 5–6, 1958–9.
2. 'Les six de jazz', *American Composers' Alliance Bulletin*, Peggy Glanville-Hicks.
3. *Palestine Post*, 20 Feb. 1959.
4. *Philadelphia Inquirer*, 5 March 1958.
5. Peggy Glanville-Hicks in interview with author, 1989.
6. *Time*, 1 Sept. 1969.
7. *Variety*, New York City, 30 Aug. 1961.
8. *Variety* magazine, US, Aug. 1961.
   Frankfurter Allgemeine Zeitung, Germany, 31 Aug. 1961.
   Le Messager D'Athenes, Aug. 1961.
   Le Figaro, France, Aug. 1961.
   Athens News, Aug. 1961.
   Musical America, Oct. 1961.
   Kathimerini, Athens, Greece, Aug. 1961.
   Daily Post, Athens, Greece, Aug. 1961.
   Arkadinos, Athens, Greece, Aug. 1961.
   London *Times*, 28 Aug. 1961.
   Guardian, England, 29 Aug. 1961.
   Time magazine, Aug. 1961.

GREECE

Following the success of the Athens Festival, Peggy felt she had earned a rest. She began to decorate her Athens house and with the proceeds from the performance began looking for a second house. She had befriended Lily Kristenson, an artist neighbour in Athens. Lily took Peggy on a day trip with her to the island of Mikonos and Peggy instantly adored it. Mikonos was a picturesque sleepy fishing village with traditional white stucco buildings, winding stone pathways and windmills on the mountainside with little thatched roofs and spinning propellers. Old men sat in cafe shopfronts by the sea drinking ouzo and coffee, and donkeys walked the streets laden with hay. The sky was a clear blue, and the white light in the afternoon reminded her of an Australian summer.

Lily, who was married at the time, spoke of an ideal life— one where the summer months were spent on the island and the colder winter months in Athens (a lifestyle not at all uncommon among wealthier Athenians). In time both women achieved their ideal. Lily rented two houses and Peggy was able to purchase a second home.

In Mikonos Peggy had discovered an abandoned pigeon house. There are a great many of these stone buildings on the Greek islands. Often the towers stand alone, their facade a complex of stone lace grille work leading to an inner room, with walls pitted by rows of pigeonholes for nesting birds. Sometimes the turrets stand beside the bare white cubes of the houses, elaborated like the towers of early Gothic churches. Or else the bird chambers will be above the houses so that the pigeons live upstairs and the people downstairs, with an outside staircase connecting the two apartments. The particular pigeon house Peggy was interested in was a latticed structure, surrounded by a beautiful solid stone wall. With

her mother's architectural eye Peggy imagined the transform-
ation that was possible.

However, even in the sixties properties were not easy to
acquire as a non-Greek. Laws governing the sale of island
properties were exclusive and complex. Peggy found a female
lawyer, Hariclia Zannou, who was sympathetic to the
problems she was facing, and returned with her to Mikonos
where the purchase of the house was negotiated. Having an
Athenian lawyer was advantageous.

Properties in the Greek islands were traditionally owned
by women. It was the woman's brother or father who were
responsible for purchasing a home, but the title and deeds
went into the name of the woman. This proved a useful basis
for the lawyer to work from. In divorce or separation the
property remains with the woman, who also keeps the
children. This pattern of ownership, which is apparently still
common, gives women a strong power base; some would even
say it borders on matriarchy.

Peggy laughed at this state of affairs and was pleased that
female ownership was not the problem besetting her. Rather
it was her foreign citizenship. Hariclia Zannou had only
recently graduated and Peggy was her first client. It was typical
of Peggy to be at the beginning of things; whether it was
a world premiere of an opera or a first appearance for a viola
player, she always enjoyed a launch. She enjoyed it all the
more if success was imminent. With her strong face and sharp
mind, Hariclia Zannou appealed to Peggy. At first meeting
she appeared sweet and malleable, but in law her ability to
tackle difficult or problematic cases made her a force. She
and Peggy became good friends and together succeeded in
organising the purchase of the beautiful pigeon house.

A great connoisseur of fine art, Peggy liked to collect
cornices of ancient beauty, Greek pottery and elegant artefacts.
Her love and respect for Greek culture and art were given
expression in her reconstruction of the pigeon house. She had
gained considerable experience in restoration while working
on her Athens home. She organised a Mikonos builder to

erect the original cornices she had found at a nearby building site, and had them positioned on the house's upper frontage. Mihalis, the builder she engaged, was to become very special to Peggy and she later described him in an unpublished short story as 'a six foot blond with sea-blue eyes, lean, handsome and proud, he grew up on Delos where his father grazed great herds, and something of the joyous solitude of Apollo's Island still clings to him.'

Mihalis suggested that a well for the water supply be dug. It was first necessary to consult with one of the local experts in this area. Konstandi arrived with a forked twig from an olive tree and marched up the hill, walking backwards and forwards in deep concentration, until the twig grew tensile in his hand. The well was dug with accurate results.

The pigeon house had to be rebuilt in sections and Mihalis was a dedicated worker. Seaweed insulation was collected, walls reshaped and mended, and stone collected from local quarries. Peggy was careful to remain loyal to tradition. Her one departure was in the tiling for the kitchen. For this she had white marble tiles with black corners manufactured after a design she had admired in an old mansion in Athens. It later transpired that this very style had been used by the old sea captains who had once lived on the island of Mikonos. She had not infringed Mikonos aesthetic after all!

When the house was complete she took a caïque to Delos before sunrise and climbed Mt Kynthos to give thanks to Apollo as the sun rose. There she placed an offering, just as she had done some months before when she was searching for a house to buy. She moved into the house at the time of a full moon, and began preparations for the long awaited house-warming party that later became something of a legend in the village. In attendance were seventy-five workmen and their wives and families, another twenty or more gatecrashers, and some travellers from an American yacht which came into the harbour that night. Two lambs were roasted on the spit and the wine that continued to arrive was lowered into the well for cooling. Peggy took care of the music with the best bouzouki players she could muster, one of whom was her sweet builder Mihalis. The sounds of santouri, bouzouki, tsambouna, and drums accompanied this jubilant gathering until the last of the guests staggered back down the hill at dawn.

A short time after Mihalis was employed to lead a team of builders in restoring the house of violinist Yehudi Menuhin. Yudee, as Peggy called him, was enthusiastic about Greece. Peggy had selected the house Yehudi purchased. No doubt he had been persuaded by her that Greece was the perfect place to rest after the exhaustion of a concert season in New York. On completion of the Menuhin house, Yehudi, his wife Diana, Peggy and Mihalis set off by boat to the island of Delos to give the traditional Greek thanksgiving. Mihalis took a gun along with him in the hope of killing a bird to take home for dinner. He shot an owl by mistake and with a look of terror on his face, brought the wounded bird to Peggy, repeating over and over that he would be doomed to bad luck because the owl was Athena's symbol.

Peggy bundled up the owl and sailed back to Mikonos with the bird shivering in her picnic basket. It had been badly injured about its head and wings but Peggy was determined that it should live. She gathered lizards and worms, which it gobbled with great gusto. She even fooled the owl into eating spaghetti in place of worms when she ran out. 'The owl couldn't tell the difference!' Peggy said.

As the weeks passed the owl recovered, but when Peggy placed him out at night to take his leave he would fly back again. One night he did disappear, but reappeared three nights later while Peggy was out. She returned to find him swinging gleefully in the chandelier, his lemon eyes gleaming like headlights. Her parakeets were shrieking with terror. She poured a drink and laughed to herself. The house, it seemed, was to be a bird house after all.

The owl remained a symbol in her life, and featured in all her homes. Friends frequently bought her miniature owl statues as gifts; and her houses became littered with them.

The owl was known to the Romans as *strix*, which means witch. The ancient Greeks believed the owl was sacred to Athena as a symbol of the wisdom of the goddess. In Christian legend the owl is one of three disobedient sisters who defied God and were transformed into birds who never looked at the sun.[1]

Mihalis, whose surname is unknown, became a devotee of Peggy's. He followed her instructions to return to Athens, where she set him to work restoring her other house. Peggy's personality gave her a curious power over people. She was at ease giving orders, but she did it in such a way that many people longed to please her. Mihalis, although married, was something of a Don Juan in his village and was known to entertain single women—and unhappily married ones—with his good cheer and eagerness to build. Reliable and willing builders were not easy to find. Mihalis was also, according to local gossip, decidedly handsome.

Mihalis enjoyed the discussions and planning of the renovations with Peggy. They could talk endlessly of design aesthetics, shape and colour. As a consequence Mihalis spent all his free time with Peggy and a delightful affair ensued. She enjoyed his company, but it was never a binding affection. Peggy knew of his reputation, but while they planned and built, he was happy to be both employee and lover. Peggy's Greek significantly improved during her time with Mihalis. Some said Mihalis learnt a great deal from Peggy. Like many Greek builders he was skilled in a range of traditional building methods, but rarely explored the full extent of his capabilities. It was believed by a number of people that Peggy's enthusiasm and aptitude for architecture raised Mihalis' status from builder to master builder. Others said that Peggy merely uncovered his talent. Either way, Mihalis ventured on, restoring and designing many more houses after his affair with Peggy had ceased. It is not clear when the affair faded; probably when his wife summoned him home as she was occasionally inclined to do; or perhaps it was the result of Peggy's many absences, her return trips to New York.

Peggy's homes became such works of art that they featured in editions of *Vogue*. This impressed Peggy's friends from all around the world who now wrote to her and begged to visit. Her houses symbolised success in her new life. As a frustrated set designer, at last she was able to have an impact. By her second summer in Greece, the Mikonos house was ready for occupation and as Peggy put it, 'The pigeons were thrown out and she, the parakeets and the owl moved in.'

The Harkness Ballet Company commissioned her while she lived in Greece to write the music for a ballet *A Season in Hell*. This ballet was based on a poem by Rimbaud entitled, *Une saison en enfer*. It was choreographed by John Butler with a cast of three and a chorus of dancers. Rimbaud was played by actor Lawrence Rhodes. The set was designed by Rouben Ter Arutunian and included an interesting backdrop—'a sort of Milky Way with steel wires in front of it'.[2] Photographs depict the dancers as spiritual nymphlike creatures, creating a fairytale atmosphere.

It opened in New York to appreciative audiences, many of whom commented on the spectacle of the dance and the choreography, unaware of their seduction by the invisible composer. Peggy kept the associated trip to New York brief and hurried back to Mikonos to enjoy the summer weather.

Peggy made several trips of this type throughout the year— her homecomings being noted by the local Greek villagers. She would be seen trudging up the dusty hill carrying exotic birds in cane birdcages, her black and red cape (extremely odd attire in a Greek summer) flowing out behind her in the wind. 'Penn-gy,' the Greeks would call, unable to manage 'Peggy'. 'Penn-gy, how was America?' they would ask, as if she had just returned from the moon. She would laugh and jangle along with her birdcages to her little home. Quick-moving in all things, she would dart up the hill; her speed always a source of amusement to her friends.

By 1963 Peggy's funds needed replenishing after all the

refurbishments to her houses, not to mention the money spent acquiring paintings or Greek pottery. An opera commission made under a grant from the Ford Foundation that year prompted a visit from English author Lawrence Durrell. Durrell was known for his books on Greece and his highly successful novel *The Alexandria Quartet*. He was no stranger to Greece, and it seemed to Peggy as if he had evoked it for the Western world with his books and stories.

As early as 1960, when work had consumed every waking hour of Peggy's time, she had written a friendly letter to Durrell. The letter had requested the rights to make an opera of his play *Sappho*. Durrell barely hesitated. His play had not received the airing it should have, and he was happy to meet with her and discuss ideas for a libretto. It took Peggy three more years to secure the necessary grant to pursue the work with Durrell. It was scheduled for an opera season in San Francisco in 1965. Durrell was to be paid $500.

Durrell's visit to Mikonos was a joyous one. Larry, as he was known to friends, spent the evening playing jazz at the piano while classicist Peggy winced. But his exuberance was so infectious that she joined in singing. (Before becoming a writer, Durrell had worked as a jazz pianist in a London nightclub called The Blue Peter.) That evening the two smoked and drank and talked until the early hours of the morning and had an argument concerning Durrell's reference to the 'English Death'—the sterility of contemporary English life. Peggy thought him overly pessimistic and critical of the English race.

His first novel, *The Black Book*, she had read long before their meeting. This work chronicles the day-to-day existence of the denizens of the Hotel Regina, a misshapen collection of unhappy loners who are spiritually dead and unable to love. He had created a sterile wasteland of British society. If all this seemed a little grim for the Australian composer who had been nurtured by old England, he redeemed himself for her in other works. Peggy retained a loyalty to England because of her fortunate start in music there at the Royal

College of Music. She also spoke of England's decline, but was probably offended by Durrell's disrespect and mockery.

Durrell's *The Alexandria Quartet*, a monumental four-part novel, is based loosely on the theory of relativity: the first three volumes deal with the theme spatially while the fourth represents it using time. Separate yet related, these four volumes sought a language to express an unknowable reality. Peggy was fascinated by *The Alexandria Quartet*. She herself conceived of a theory of unifying time and space within music. She wanted to express in music new depths, to find types of rhythms which were universal.

For Durrell, modern man and woman are ultimately alone, at the mercy of their desires in a swiftly changing reality in which nothing is really as it seems. None is exempt from passion, yet almost all are denied any fulfilment. These and a host of other ideas including the maturation of the artist made the evening memorable. Were it not for his brash playing of jazz music Peggy might well have met the man of her dreams. There was continued banter between the two about his taste for jazz and her secret passion for detective novels.

Durrell returned home after several days with Peggy on Mikonos, to continue work on *An Irish Faustus*, which was due for publication in late 1963. His letters during their correspondence about *Sappho* tell of this period, and convey his loneliness: 'I do an hour of yoga and poke about in the guts of a new novel.' Faber and Faber were wanting him to promote a new paperback edition of *The Alexandria Quartet*. The libretto of *Sappho* was completed by 1964. Yehudi Menuhin had settled into his house nearby and Peggy had written to Durrell of his presence. Durrell did not meet Menuhin during his visit, but Peggy wrote to him of Yehudi's successes. When Peggy's manuscript of *Sappho* was completed it was delivered in person to the music publisher, Alder in New York, by Menuhin.

The story of Sappho appealed to Peggy because of its pre-occupation with the feminine in Greek mythology. Sappho was the poet and priestess of Lesbos, the isle of women. She married and had one daughter, Cleis, and devoted her later life to the love of women. She was called the tenth muse and was much revered. Most of her books had been burned or destroyed throughout the ages, only a very few fragments of her poetry surviving. Ruled by women, Lesbos was devoted to the service of Aphrodite and Artemis, and the practice of grace, or *charis*, as it is called by the Greeks. This grace refers to the practice of music, art, dancing, poetry, philosophy and romantic lesbian love.[3] Durrell had been fascinated by the idea of the feminine side of the male character, the anima. He named his daughter Sappho, which means, simply, poetess.

A production of *Sappho* did not seem to be forthcoming. The San Francisco company which in 1963 had given Peggy eighteen months to complete the work, brought the deadline forward. It was their intention to have Maria Callas take the lead but she broke the contract. This was a big disappointment for Peggy, who had long wanted to write a piece for the gifted singer.

Correspondence between Durrell and Peggy also suggests that there were some disagreements between them during the process. In one letter he said, 'Do whatever you like, it's your play.' In another letter he mentioned his sympathy for her bout of illness—trouble that she was experiencing with her eyes. A third letter outlined their differences over *Sappho* as being mere technicalities, and yet he declined to permit a production. Peggy's letters indicated that the differences were related specifically to his unwillingness to cut any of the text. ' "But that's my favourite line," he would say—about every line,' Peggy said. She felt there was too much recitative. Some type of stalemate must have occurred. At the completion of the score Peggy was dissatisfied because she believed the opera was too long and needed editing. Durrell was happy because every word had found a home.

Whatever the value of the piece, its fate was sealed. The work never received a single performance. As late as 1972 the Adelaide Festival in Australia sought to produce the work but was unsuccessful. Peggy always believed that the length of the piece made it too expensive to produce. But perhaps the lesbian content of the material failed to appeal.

Sappho was doomed not because of anything Lawrence Durrell was to do, but because within three years Peggy was to experience a blow to her career that she would never really recover from. 'I just knew something was wrong with me but you know, it didn't fit in with my career plans,' Peggy said. Subconsciously she had already prepared herself for a slower pace by purchasing the houses in Greece. During the production of *Nausicaa* journalists had recorded significant details concerning Peggy's health. Interestingly enough these clippings were nowhere to be found in her personal folders, where she kept all music and personal notices.

Time had described *Nausicaa* as Peggy's second-last work, citing *Sappho* as the finale because 'her eyes, overtaxed by years of reading and music copying, are failing badly, and she fears eventual blindness'.[4] The London *Times* said: 'P.G.-H. will have to stop writing music because of worsening eyesight.'[5] She was quoted as saying, 'There are a couple more works which I want to write before this condition overtakes me. One of them is a big opera of the play *Sappho* by Lawrence Durrell.' She went on: 'While not experiencing complete blindness, I have extreme long-sightedness which makes it impossible to focus on anything as close as a music desk.' She chided the interviewer, 'When I first arrived in Mikonos I was able to see the fleas on the goats on the next island.'

The *Daily Telegraph* and *Morning Post* in Australia described her as 'accepting her pending blindness'.[6] They claimed that her 'eye condition was induced by years spent copying pages of other people's music to earn a living before she began writing her own'. This quote appears to have come directly from Peggy herself. In a similar vein she mused with the journalist, 'I will touch type and write books on music and aesthetics.'[7]

Despite her persistent headaches and her comments in interviews, she continued to believe that the condition was temporary.

Between 1962 and 1965 Peggy made several visits to New York to complete various contracts. Friends such as John Butler had noticed some changes in her behaviour. She appeared to be edgy, less able to communicate. Butler had always perceived her to be sociable; now he found her increasingly critical, impatient, even antisocial. In 1963 Peggy visited London briefly and consulted some doctors. Her friends in England also found her behaviour altered. They said she was living with constant headaches. Back in Greece friends who visited her had similar tales. Oliver Daniels and Don Ott, long-time friends whose company Peggy always found agreeable, were surprised by her moods. Oliver, who could tease Peggy about having boots cooking in the oven in her New York apartment, now found little humour in their meetings. Other friends felt she was becoming embittered. They rationalised that her distance from New York had thrown her into obscurity and that she envied others' successes. This is doubtful. Peggy usually made whatever choices were necessary and rarely if ever looked back.

Don Ott described his and Oliver Daniel's stay with her on Mikonos:

> After Peggy finished fixing some spouting problem she was having she instructed me to get ready and accompany her into the village. She was always climbing ladders, painting, sawing wood, sculpting a gnome for the garden. Well, she got dressed and we set off at great walking speed to one of those Mr Dropatopoloss's. When we arrived at the builder's house, Peggy asked me to assist her in picking up a huge paving stone. I was used to following her instructions. She called Mr Dropatopoloss's name and in one swift gesture heaved this huge paving stone through the front window of his workshop with shattering impact. Apparently the builder had kept postponing the job of fixing her house, hence the rock throwing.

Perhaps this incident can be explained by her ill health; perhaps the builder in question was Mihalis her former lover;

perhaps it was sheer temper. Don commented that, 'At this stage nothing had been diagnosed and I didn't know what the hell was going on but this wasn't the Peggy that Oliver and I had known in New York.'

In 1966 producer Pamela Illot was working at CBS Television, putting together cultural religious programs. She was trying to persuade Peggy to write a score for one of her programs and wrote to her in Greece. Peggy replied, mentioning an intended trip at the end of the month. She had quite a lot of work to tend to in New York: some incidental music for film, a few brief scores for television and a revival concert series with the Composers' Forum. Illot knew it would not be easy to tempt her. Peggy preferred to come up with her own ideas in music, and gossip suggested that she was more temperamental than ever. But Illot was optimistic after receiving the letter. She perceived her to be something of a feminist, and negotiated with Peggy on her arrival for a biblical ballet, *Jephthah's Daughter*. John Butler was the obvious choice for her to combine with, and they both agreed. Peggy stayed with her friends Ralph and Caroline Backlund, a couple she had befriended in the course of her work some years earlier, on Madison and 90th Street. Ralph was an important editor and founder of an early Smithsonian publication, and Caroline a senior ranking librarian.

On the ship over from Greece Peggy encountered a doctor. He listened attentively to her description of her eye trouble and frightened her with the thought that she might in fact be experiencing the effects of a brain tumour. So worried was she by this information that when she arrived in New York to stay with her friends, she visited a doctor. This doctor dispelled her fears, telling her that she was suffering severe tension and that she should take up some form of exercise such as swimming, which she did.

Jephthah's Daughter, or *Tragic Celebrations* as it was officially titled, was presented by CBS Television in 1966 as part of the Sunday morning religious program. It proved to be a popular television dance piece, and was rescheduled for further screenings. The work starred actors Buzz Miller and Carmen de Lavallade. Most of the reviews focused on Butler to the exclusion of the actors and the composer.

The story was taken from the Bible and told of Jephthah, the Gileadite, who overcame the Ammonites after pledging to God the sacrifice of the first person he met on his return from the battlefield, only to find that this was his beloved only child. The conflict of love and duty provided all the impetus needed for dance and music. The *New York Times* reviewed it in 1966, attributing the success of the piece to 'the choreography and direction coming together with unpretentiously effective music by Peggy Glanville-Hicks—a cohesive unity that dance on television rarely achieves'. Butler was praised for his 'seamless choreography'.[8]

When the production was over, Butler asked Peggy to join him and a friend on an outing to the beach for a weekend. She accepted, believing a short break would reduce the tension she was experiencing. Her eye condition seemed to improve over that weekend. The term Peggy used for John Butler and his friend was 'riotous company'. Stimulating conversation and clever wit picked up her spirits. She and John even spoke of menopause and lost romantic chances, as well as her new life in Greece, and the weighing up of professional choices. Peggy seemed happy with her decision to live in Greece but John doubted her. They also discussed the new opera she had written just before *Jephthah's Daughter*, entitled *The Glittering Gate*. It was showing in New York. Designed as a curtain raiser, a mini-opera in one act, it was easily programmed with other work. The text was written by Lord Dunsany and the opera was composed for tenor, chamber orchestra and electronic tape. Just thirty minutes in duration, the opera was proving quite a success.

Her weekend with Butler relieved her momentarily from the Composers' Forum where she was involved in a series of follow-up concerts. Despite having left the directorship some five or six years previously, she was still tossing ideas at them from Greece. This recent visit found her promoting revivals of work such as *Ballet Mécanique* by George Antheil, Concerto for Piano and Wind Octet by Colin McPhee, as well as a Paul Bowles opera, *The Wind Remains*. All of these works had been neglected for years and Peggy was eager to re-run them. As before, her production skills were called upon and she was a willing collaborator. Towards the end of the fifties she had gained financial backing, using the title 'The Artists' Company' for a revival of the opera *Rapunzel*, by Lou Harrison. This work had earlier been awarded the Twentieth-century Masterpiece Prize in Rome but was unknown in the USA. This success endeared her to the Composers' Forum and accounted for her active role, yet again, in revival work.

This was no time to be feeling unwell. Peggy and Butler were enjoying their stay at Fire Island, a place referred to by local residents as 'the pines'. Peggy had visited there a few times before, and always appreciated the change of scenery, but on this occasion the journey back to New York took a different turn. John was driving and Peggy began to complain about the fog. She complained that she could only see the red tail-lights of the cars ahead. 'Giovanni,' she said, 'pull over, it's too dangerous to drive under these conditions.' Butler pulled to the side lane and stopped. 'Peggy love, there is no fog,' he said. She must have realised her error because of his puzzled face and she spoke hurriedly, 'Giovanni, I'm going blind. I can only see little red dots.' Her terror increased, as did the blindness, and Butler drove her immediately to her friends the Backlunds.

As they arrived Butler became aware of Peggy's urgent condition. She stepped off the kerb to enter the apartment block and was almost run down. He got her into the apartment and Ralph Backlund rang an eye specialist and explained Peggy's condition. Dr Trautman was distinguished in his field and therefore difficult to obtain an appointment with. Ralph's urgency convinced the doctor, and appointments were juggled, with Trautman agreeing to see her at 8 a.m. the following day. Three hours after Peggy's consultation, Ralph Backlund received a telephone call from the doctor explaining the seriousness of Peggy's condition. Her worst fears were confirmed. She had a brain tumour.

John Butler, who had been waiting fearfully for the news, drove Peggy from the doctor's clinic to the Columbia Presbyterian Memorial Hospital in Harlem, where she was admitted. Within hours Ralph Backlund received a second telephone call, this time from the hospital. It was explained to him that the patient had no health insurance and therefore such expensive surgery could not be initiated without proof of her ability to pay. Peggy was taken to what was referred to as a charity room, where non-financial patients were placed until a course of action could be decided. Although X-rays and tests showed that the tumour was benign, it posed a life-threatening risk because of its size and the degree of internal swelling. It was described as the size of a small orange, enmeshed within other brain sections. It was obvious she was facing death without surgical intervention.

Ralph rang Peggy's friends Oliver Daniels, Isaac Stern and Yehudi Menuhin, and anyone else he could think of who might be able to assist with the cost of surgery. Everyone offered their assistance, but it was necessary for all to commit to paper their agreement to pay, and the figure had to total the exact cost before surgery could begin. Peggy lay in her hospital bed oblivious to the confusion about her. Caroline Backlund visited her after hearing the dreadful diagnosis from her husband. She recalled later that Peggy was worried, but relieved that the cause of her blindness had been diagnosed. 'Well, if this is what we have to do, let's do it, let's get on with it,' she had said, not aware of the financial holdups.

Francis Thorn, an acquaintance of Peggy's who was still living in New York, received a call from Silvia Spencer saying that Virgil Thomson had given $500 and Yehudi Menuhin $1,000 towards Peggy's operation. Thorn gave $500 also but the total sum required was more in the vicinity of $6,000. Silvia set to work raising the rest. She asked for Francis's help through the Thorn Music Fund. This fund granted three year fellowships to composers, and occasionally it could make an emergency grant. Francis was a cousin of Landon and Oakleigh Thorn, by whom he was employed, more as a favour than anything else. They were the managers of the fund so he could not exert the influence that he would have liked. Virgil Thomson, whom Thorn described as 'a great humanitarian despite his snappy personality', along with Spencer, masterminded a plan to get quick approval by putting together a panel of musical heavyweights. The distinguished panel included Aaron Copland, Peter Mennin, Gian Carlo Menotti and Douglas Moore. Francis Thorn worked with them round the clock to persuade the Thorn management to approve the money. $1,650 was granted and this along with contributions from each of the composers, as well as from Peggy's Greenwich Village friends Gore Vidal, Martha Graham (whom she knew only as a neighbour and an acquaintance) and Leonard Bernstein, made up the difference.[9]

In great haste surgery was arranged. Peggy was advised that it could result in partial or total blindness. She gave her consent. For many hours after the delicate operation she remained unconscious. John Butler sat with her throughout. She had been packed in ice in a bathtub arrangement, so that the blood flow would be slowed and the body would remain at a low temperature for four or five hours following surgery. When she began to come round, Butler heard her squeaky voice and stirred. She said: 'I'm very cold, can't you do something?' Butler was quick to retort, 'Are you complaining Peggy? Is that you complaining?' She opened her eyes and stared at the ceiling. She could just make out the design when her voice came more strongly. 'I can see! I can see perfectly!' John was in tears.

In the following three months of recuperation, Peggy stayed for a short while with the Backlunds and then moved among various friends in Greenwich Village. Her friends had organised themselves so that she could have someone with her during the day. Although she was very thin, sometimes dizzy and initially off-balance, her health began to recover. Her head had been shaved for the operation and she wore a scarf as soon as the bandages were removed. One afternoon Gore Vidal, Tennessee Williams and Martha Graham arrived at her doorstep in Greenwich Village on a surprise visit and took her by taxi to a theatre props store. Without laughing they dragged her to the counter. Peggy stood there with them, completely perplexed as to the purpose of their visit. 'We've all come to hire a wig.' The boy behind the counter was awed by the artistic giants, and hurried out to find the wigs. They could hear him calling for the boss, who was nowhere to be found. Everyone began to laugh. The trying on of wigs caused even greater delight, and when they had finally settled on their choices, they set off to a cafe sporting their new hairstyles. Peggy's choice was the only tasteful one.

When she regained her strength New York began presenting her with new problems. Funding for the arts was in a state of turmoil with much political debate. And while arguments between sponsors continued, artistic areas suffered. She engaged in a few wrangles with funding officials over the Composers' Forum. But this was not her fight any more, no longer being director. There was also conflict amongst Peggy's artistic rivals as well who were now back to their normal bitching and complaining about her receipt of funding for projects in the past as well as more general artistic jealousies. There had been a move away from the funding of composers by leading arts benefactors. They were now investing huge quantities of money in technology; the synthesiser had been born and the new electronic music of the future was expensive. Peggy was exhausted and depressed by all of these changes. She planned to slip quietly back to Greece.

After three months her hair had started to grow back, although not enough to show off in polite society, she felt. Caroline Backlund arranged to get Peggy's special medications sent to her in Greece from New York, and in her usual economical style Peggy made arrangements to board a freighter for Athens. Her recovery seemed miraculous, and yet when she visited her practitioner for what was to be the last time before departing for Greece his words came slowly and deliberately. He explained to her that although she seemed well now and apparently recovering, after such radical surgery she could only expect to live four to five years. Peggy reeled in shock! She shouted a blur of words at him and stumbled out of his surgery into the street.

She told no-one this news and cheerily waved goodbye to friends at the dock, her eyes fixed far out to sea. She wrote postcards on board, pretending to her New York friends that there would be several works ahead. Privately she was sure of nothing.

Still holding a little of the money she had left from the *Sappho* commission and *The Glittering Gate* production, Peggy settled into her home on Mikonos. There was much to consider: her quality of life, her work, and what future she could create for herself. She visited the nearby islands by boat and spent time on the island of Delos, immersing herself in mythology and archaeology—former interests that had been neglected under the pressure of work over the last twenty years. Delos was the home of Apollo. Local villagers told her that no-one was permitted to be born on the island, nor were they ever allowed to die there. Peggy loved such stories. She returned to Delos, to Mt Kynthos, to make a wish to live. It was here that she had visited just a few years earlier to give thanksgiving for her newly acquired house.

She was attracted to the simplicity of rural Greek life on the nearby island of Tinos. After days of walking and thinking she stumbled across a little tumble-down cottage that was vacant, and the idea of renewal and rebuilding held out its irresistible appeal. She made enquiries, phoned her lawyer friend Hariclia in Athens, and purchased the dilapidated house for a small sum of money. Happy to have a new project, she returned to Mikonos, just a twenty minute ferry journey away, gathered up some essentials, and moved across to Tinos. She had vague plans of selling one of the other two properties at a later date, but for now a paint can and the hunt for a capable builder was enough.

The Tinos house resembled a cottage one might expect to find in Cornwall. Situated high above the village of Kardiani, it perched like an eagle's nest overlooking the ocean in the distance. In Kardiani the natural browns and greys of the slate work are regarded with reverence. Important stone is not whitewashed. In Peggy's little home, alcoves were shaved away to make room for a bookshelf or a cupboard, or simply to make an ideal space to hang a basket. Like an ever-changing sculpture the house was shaped to fit her needs. At the front of the house, a terrace overlooked the Aegean. The silence, she said, made it possible for her to hear music.

On my visit to Tinos in 1989 I heard the same echoing of words and phrases in the wind. In this stillness there were no human voices, no song; just the sound of the wind, the view of an eagle. At this distance from the sea there was only colour, the turquoise baby blue, the rich purple-blood-blue, the hazy silver-blue and then the dusty white-blue, a sea lifting into the sky with no horizon. The opera *Sappho* reflects this vision, this colourful silence. Peggy had rewritten some of the music of the *Sappho* score here in this house. She had felt from the first day she entered the house that it would be an ideal place to write music, her special place.

As biographer this is the one time I lingered, staying in her house. I sat in the brilliant white light of Greece that Peggy had so often described to me. The house's curves and alcoves had become familiar to me. I moved the desk and chair by the window to write as she might have done. When I looked out of the window I would dream. I felt the identification that readers might imagine yet also had the separateness of the biographer's eye. The surly winds of Tinos pulled threads in the ocean's blanket and little white pull-marks appeared on the surface. In calm weather, these threads would be pulled to the other side of the island and the sea would again appear smooth. Could Peggy have witnessed such images or was I redreaming everything?

As with Mikonos, Peggy's eccentricities endeared her to the village people on Tinos. As the only foreigner to be living in Kardiani, her habits were closely observed. Her house was geographically at the top of the village, which is shaped into the hillside. One day she was seen scattering packets of flower seeds down the mountainside in the early hours of the morning, and the following summer the most fantastic blooms began to appear in vivid colours. Peggy stared out with pride at her handiwork from her slate grey balcony. The village women gossiped, but everyone admired the flowers.

With little else to occupy her socially during the winter months she befriended the local taxi driver Mihalis, or 'number two', as she jokingly referred to him, distinguishing him from Mihalis on Mikonos. Mihalis drove a rather dilapidated old Mercedes Benz. He proved to be of great assistance during her move to Tinos, ferrying all of her belongings from the boat. The house was about twenty minutes drive from the wharf, but as Mihalis's car was prone to burning oil, the journey could sometimes take even longer. He was a dutiful friend who would move furniture around the house for her. He would spend a dusty day gardening with her or ferreting for discarded ceramic pots in the outer villages. Sometimes they shopped at the nearby village of Pyrgos for fruit, vegetables and freshly baked bread. Mihalis was an asset when it came to negotiating a price for produce. It is quite common for Greek men to do the shopping and for the 'foreigner woman', as she was sometimes referred to, this meant a saving. Mihalis would drive her to and fro like a chauffeur.

Together they created a small garden of geraniums, poppies, an occasional rose and a wide array of Peggy's favoured purple-blue flowers. In the evenings they would sit out on the grey slate balcony protected from the fierce winds by the large wooden side door that she had especially designed and Mihalis had built. In cold months the expanse of sea turned icy-blue. The moon was a hard white light in a black sky. Mihalis was happy to be in the company of such a refined lady who not only prepared sumptuous casseroles and salads, but whose skill at the piano surpassed any he had ever heard. Their affair was simple and sweet and brought Peggy a degree of comfort. Mihalis learned to speak a little English from Peggy and in turn he taught her Greek. She would write down all the descriptive words, including verbs that she thought she would most often need, and in the evenings after dinner, sitting out in the night air, they would practise together. The affair however did not last as Peggy grew tired of her unequal intellectual comrade. In any case too serious a liaison might threaten her independence and she was not about to share her house with a partner.

So Mihalis drifted out and visitors from overseas drifted in. Her house restorations developed slowly, and in time another man appeared on the scene. Nickiphorus Bidalis was a builder in Kardiani who had lived in the village all his life. Like Mihalis number one, he was a naturally gifted builder who loved the architect in Peggy, and together they rebuilt sections of the Tinos house. Peggy enjoyed the company of Bidalis. He was humorous, warm and affectionate—and a careful worker.

On one of her outings with Bidalis Peggy found a large metal griffin partly buried in the soil and hurried home for digging implements. When they unearthed the piece it was enmeshed with corroded pieces of metal. Her eyes lit up with satisfaction as the large mythical creature came to the surface, perfectly intact! She knew he belonged above her gate on the Tinos house, and he was installed there, a symbol to distinguish her house from all the others. The griffin is said to keep away evil spirits, and given the tranquillity of her life in the Tinos house he definitely did his job.

Peggy preferred to remain aloof from the Kardiani village people, with the exception of shopping expeditions and the purchase of necessary building materials. She claimed that she loved the Greeks and respected them, but other than her lovers she never fraternised with them. Perhaps she didn't want to pretend to be something she knew she was incapable of being. She never got involved socially, but her distance brought with it a mutual respect, the respect of unfamiliarity.

Peggy enjoyed the solitude of Tinos and avoided most company. Her closest friend in Greece, the painter Lily Kristenson, had recently moved to Mikonos and was busy using hand-loomed materials in her new collage works. Lily depicted village life in the islands. She and her husband lived a short distance from Peggy's Mikonos house, and when Peggy was there the two women saw each other frequently. Lily also stayed with Peggy on Tinos, usually bringing her small child with her.

Peggy, although not a trained painter herself, had an almost obsessive eye for colour and design. She created one or two paintings which were particularly impressive for a novice. With Lily she could discuss the colours of Greece: the greys and browns of the landscape, the blues and whites of the houses—so like the colour of the sea. The sunsets were dusty pink set in mauve-blue skies, and the many tones of white were unique to this part of the world. 'A white sun,' Peggy would say, as if no-one had ever noticed before. She liked to convince Lily that her impressions were superior.

Lily recalled Peggy's opinions on dress, and how she liked to tell people which colour they were missing. 'Perfection was Peggy's domain,' Lily said. Peggy usually advised others in a positive tone, although she was not averse to commenting in a negative manner if she knew the person well. At the same time her generosity would lead her to dig into her cupboards and drawers to find the scarf or bow-tie that would best suit someone's outfit. These she happily gave to the person in question, no doubt believing that the next time she saw them they would not offend her with their inadequate sense of style. Fortunately most of her comments were appreciated. Whenever she won a battle of design with a friend she would laugh heartily and affectionately hug them.

Lily thought of Peggy as a frustrated costume designer. She designed and made her own clothes, especially during leaner years, and was known to construct an outfit, sewing by hand, if a fabric so inspired her. In New York she had previously had clothes designed for her on opening nights by a range of gifted clothing designers, one being the famous Schiaparelli. In New York she had been photographed by Man Ray for a biographical brochure, wearing her Schiaparelli outfit. She told Lily how she and Schiaparelli had shared discussion on line, form, design, light and colour. She believed good taste could be acquired, but being born with a natural sense of design and architecture she overlooked the possibility that all persons were not as interested in such matters as she.

When Lily gave birth to her second child, Peggy seemed shocked by this event. Obviously she had not paid too much attention to the painter's changing waistline, they had rarely discussed the pregnancy and so its conclusion came as a surprise to Peggy. Lily considered it quite typical of Peggy to overlook matters of physical reproduction, but still she held no doubt that Peggy cared for her.

During an interview in 1989 on the island of Mikonos, Lily and I walked around the ruins of the house she and her husband had once lived in. It was only a few yards downhill from Peggy's house. Lily remembered the birth. While her husband played guitar with friends in the next room she lay on her bed in labour. She could hear the chatter and drinking, the merriment, while she waited for a new life to appear. It had been an extremely hot day and her body was saturated with perspiration. Lily was a foreigner and the local Greek women normally didn't speak to her, but birth brought compassion. During the day of labour, they threw flowers through her window. Lily described the house as collapsing. White bloodied doves burst from the walls and took flight as her wails brought forth a shiny baby boy. Her husband continued to play guitar and sing loudly in Spanish in the next room, heedless of the miracles Lily was performing in the bedroom, alone.

After the birth the younger Greek mothers came to visit her. Peggy also came to visit. Peggy was never particularly fond of children; she had never really known any, and was both a help and a hindrance, according to Lily. She would help with the peeling of vegetables in preparation for a meal and she would vaguely tidy up, hiding an item or two from sight to create a more orderly effect. She seemed to know very little about responding to the needs of small children. She didn't understand that they had to be socialised first, and would sometimes talk over the top of the children's cries for attention. Mostly children irritated her by their uneven temperament and limited ability to communicate politely. Still, Peggy remained loyal and warm to Lily, whom she saw as an artist trapped in domesticity. When Lily's new child was still quite young her Spanish husband deserted her.

Peggy passed the four- to five-year sentence during which she had expected to die from some tumour-related seizure. One day when she was not particularly thinking of her former illness she asked Bidalis the date. He answered her in Greek and she began to laugh. Perplexed, he asked what it was that had made her so happy. In an enigmatic way she said: 'I've been twiddling my fingers for years and now it hasn't happened. I'm going to live!' she dashed about the balcony singing and poured a generous glass of brandy which she splashed theatrically on the ground, 'To Apollo,' she sang, 'god of medicine and the arts. He is on my side.'

In 1971 Peggy received a letter from her brother Beric saying his son Roger was coming to visit her. Roger Glanville-Hicks was twenty-one years old and had childhood memories of his eccentric aunt whom he remembered from family picnics at Mount Martha in Victoria. He had been an enthusiastic young guitar player of fourteen when his aunt Peggy, who was said by those at home to be gallivanting around the world, offered to write a letter of introduction to the famous Spanish guitarist Andrés Segovia on his behalf. Segovia was then working and living between Sienna and California. He had made a considerable contribution to the twentieth century revival of the guitar as a concert instrument, and a great many composers had written works for him. Roger did receive an offer from him but was too young to consider leaving school and home. Peggy had overlooked this detail.

By 1971 Roger had completed a music degree in Melbourne and wanted to study abroad. His trip by ship took six weeks, just as Peggy's had in 1932. It proved to be quite dramatic, with a cyclone hitting just off the coast near Cape Town. This was Roger's first trip abroad and Peggy waited anxiously at the wharf in Piraeus for her young relative to arrive. It was strangely exciting for both of them.

Roger, seated beside her in a Greek taxi was stunned when the vehicle took off at a roaring speed. He heard his aunt scream at the driver in a shocking tone, 'Cigar, cigar,' meaning slowly, slowly. Oblivious, the taxi took another gravelled curve at a speed that would have frightened Odysseus. Arriving at the Athens house Roger was struck by its beauty. In the terracotta-coloured living room were Etruscan prints, copies from the first photographs taken when the tombs in Etruria had been opened. On adjacent walls were masks of Apollo and Dionysus. Her home was a marvel of interesting Greek artefacts and myths. Her pottery was delicate and each piece carried an extraordinary story. Roger was fascinated, and that night he drank brandy with his aunt, sitting out on the back porch of the house at the foot of the Acropolis. The Parthenon was lit against a soft grey evening sky, and in the warm air this seemed like paradise to Roger.

In the months that followed Roger was privy to the smallest details of Peggy's life. They did everything together: shopping, building, gardening, visiting friends. Peggy, according to Roger, was not writing any music at all. He could not imagine when she would have found time. An endless stream of visitors passed through from New York and Europe, and life seemed like a continuous party with drinks at 'elevenses' and 'fiveses', Peggy's words for drinks time. Roger soon found himself drinking more than he ever had before and taking the mandatory nap after lunch.

He was forever trying to keep up with his aunt, not only

in drinking, but also in simple shopping ventures. Peggy would be way out in front with Roger following at a quick pace. He noticed her need to be first in all things: first on the ferry so as to get a good seat, and first off the ferry so as to get home. His speedy aunt would negotiate her way through the crowded fish markets of Athens while Roger would be left behind among the Greeks competing for a good price. He described his aunt as 'rude to people', a quality in her which both offended and amused. But he was impressed by her command of Greek, and like many before him, soon fell under her spell, responding to instructions with the same obedience and willingness as other friends.

Peggy was able, by this stage, to survive financially on royalties. She had agreed during her illness in New York to have a flat rate of income calculated by Broadcast Music Incorporated that was averaged over the year's earnings. Whenever Peggy's music was heard on radio, film or television a fee would normally be forwarded to her. Broadcast Music Incorporated managed these royalty collections. In some instances Peggy would lose money, especially when a large production company was using her music. But averaging it over time gave her the security of knowing she would always have approximately four to five thousand pounds a year. This was adjusted annually to keep in line with inflation. The real advantage of this money came in later life when the composer had next to nothing being broadcast. In a sense it was a type of superannuation, sustaining a comfortable life in Greece.

Peggy loved beautiful bathrooms and during Roger's stay in Athens she arranged for a builder to install a new bath she had acquired. Shortly after the builder started digging he struck a hard surface. He uncovered a huge marble foot which was attached to a perfectly formed leg. Following the marble line, a torso was partly unearthed. Peggy recoiled in horror at the sight of it and ordered the builder to replace the soil. Her panic was brought on by the possibility that her house might be torn down by archaeological zealots. Only a hundred yards from the foot of the Acropolis, it was highly likely that the entire block was a treasure of ancient relics. She instructed the builder to remain quiet and dig a second hole on the opposite side of the room. The bath was put in place and the discussion dropped.

Peggy enjoyed her young nephew's stay. At night he would play his guitar in the hallway as she lay in bed, and by day it was possible to talk about music if the mood so took her.

Roger's discussions with Peggy on music in America led him to believe she was embittered. Electronic music had arrived. It was much more difficult for her to raise interest or money in the way she had before in New York. With the advent of the magnetic tape, compositions were now reaching a world audience, but with this came the technology that was to change the face of music and composition forever. According to Roger, Peggy hated this new technology. She felt musically harmed by it. It became a block that prevented her working again. The thought of fighting in New York for funding for composers was one thing, but the battle against technology was a fight against the future, one that Peggy realised she could not win.

In an article for *Vogue* titled 'Tapesichord' Peggy wrote that the new musical technology confused noise with sound. She cited her friend John Cage as one of those who wanted to legitimise odd materials into aural compositions. 'He is at present setting up a library of canned supplies—if one may mix metaphors—of already recorded music to be purchasable by the yard or the minute.' Although she was not hostile about electronic music in this article, she cleverly drew distinctions between noises and sounds throughout. She talked to Roger of her inability to 'approach music' in the way she had before. It had grown away from her somehow. At times she was hostile to his attitude, which favoured integrating the new technology.

Roger's parents arrived in Greece towards the end of the year. Roger's visit had brought her closer to her family again, after years of believing she could live quite well without them. Beric, for whom she always had a great affection, had visited her in New York and this visit to Greece made the ties even stronger. Former conflicts were put behind them, and Beric's wife Paddy and Peggy made up their differences. Paddy Glanville-Hicks was one of the few people to have stood up against Peggy's stubbornness and bossiness, qualities she respected her for in the long run. With renewed family connections and much news of Australia, Peggy felt for the first time a pull back towards the country she had escaped at nineteen.

One year before Roger's visit, in 1970, Peggy's opera *The Transposed Heads* had its first Australian performance at the University of New South Wales in Sydney. At the same time her Sonata for Recorder and Concertino da Camera were played at the Dallas Brooks Hall in Melbourne. Peggy had intended to return to Australia to witness these productions, but was delayed en route in London where she underwent a minor ear operation. She had visited shortly after, and had been impressed with Australia and its talented musicians and composers. She said of this visit: 'I was overwhelmed by what I found.'

Her Athens house was testament to the high hopes she had for herself in Australia. On the walls of her house she hung the pictures and plans of the new Sydney Opera House which she believed to be of supreme architectural design. She began that wishing of hers that had often led to something fruitful. It was her dream to have one of her pieces played in the Sydney Opera House.

Australia was becoming increasingly attractive to her. An arts librarian from the State Library of Victoria, Joyce McGrath, who had visited Peggy in Greece to collect music scores, said that Peggy was delighted to have her work stored in Australia. McGrath kept a diary from this visit in which she recorded Peggy as saying: 'I am homesick for that fenceless, endless dreaming landscape.' During the visit to Australia when she missed the production of *The Transposed Heads* she had said to McGrath: 'Australia . . . how the magnet pulls now that I have seen it again.' McGrath knew from that moment Peggy would come home for good.

NOTES

1. *The Woman's Encylcopedia of Myths and Secrets*, Harper and Row, US, 1983, p. 754.
2. Winthrop Sargeant, *The New Yorker*.
3. *The Woman's Encyclopedia of Myths and Secrets*, pp. 535, 890.
4. *Time*, 21 Aug. 1961.
5. London *Times*, 21 Aug. 1961.
6. *Daily Telegraph*, 7 Sept. 1961.
7. *Morning Post*, 7 Sept. 1961.
8. *New York Times*, 7 Nov. 1966.
9. Francis Thorn, in interview with the author, New York, 1989.

SYDNEY, AUSTRALIA

In 1975, the Australian Music Centre invited Peggy to give a series of lectures on Asian Music. While this was only a part-time position, the Centre was eager to find other useful ways to keep Peggy occupied. This was to be a semi-retirement role and provided her with the necessary impetus to return home. Peggy travelled to Sydney to investigate the possibilities and, after talks with the Australian Music Centre, felt confident that she would spend her future in Sydney. She arranged for the sale of her Greek houses, selling the Tinos house to her friend Lily for a reasonably small amount, reasoning that Lily now had to educate her children on a single income. The Mikonos house was sold privately.

In Sydney she combed the inner city for a suitable house. The Greek houses, for all their aesthetic beauty, brought her a relatively small amount once converted into Australian dollars. After a lengthy search she found and purchased a moderately priced house in Paddington. Paddington was then, as she said, 'on the wrong side of the road'. She chose the house for a weeping willow tree that lay at the foot of the garden. In Australia, as in Greece, she brought a brown poodle for company and began the work of establishing a home and garden, a place for inspiration.

The Australian Music Centre provided Peggy with an ideal work life. She performed lectures, gave talks, socialised and encouraged young composers. She met and made friends with many of the Australian composers who frequented the Centre. But for all this activity Peggy wrote few new compositions during this time.

In 1978, while working at the Australian Music Centre, Peggy received photographs of a new sculpture series from her friend Pamela Bowden. Peggy was so intrigued by the wooden subjects that she went to Bowden with an idea. 'What a pity sculptures can't sing' she told Bowden and explained her proposal simply. She would like to commission seven composers to compose a piece of music based on one of the seven sculptures. Bowden was delighted and agreed.

The composers were to be Don Banks, Ross Edwards, Lou Harrison, Vincent Plush, Peter Sculthorpe, David Gulpilil, and Peggy. After explaining to each composer what she wanted them to do they set to work happily, with the exception of Gulpilil. He stared at Peggy in despair, then followed behind her as she beckoned him towards the sculpture selected for him. He shook his head when she spoke of scored music and instead sat down on the floor, selected a didgeridoo from the next room and began to play. In ten minutes the piece was complete and Peggy felt it was one of the most exciting. For her own composition Peggy selected a giraffe-like sculpture and wrote *Girondelle for Giraffes*. The resulting compositions were combined as 'Seven Sculptures for Seven Compositions', and became an exhibition at the Tolarno Galleries, St. Kilda. It offered a novel audio–visual experience in which each sculpture was illuminated in sequence with its accompanying musical composition. The exhibit was a success and received a number of reviews in leading newspapers.

Peggy did not compose any further music after the Seven Sculptures project until 1986 when she began work on the opera *Becket*. The libretto of *Becket*, written by myself at her instruction, is based on the life of Thomas à Becket and traces the motivations that lead to T.S. Eliot's *Murder In the Cathedral*.

Well before this, in 1984, Peggy received an invitation to travel to Perth for a new production of *The Transposed Heads*. The production was to be recorded for broadcast on the Australian Broadcasting Commission's FM network, with singers accompanied by the West Australian Symphony Orchestra.[1] The train trip proved to be much longer than Peggy had imagined possible, but on board there was merriment and good cheer. The train across Australia to Perth is legendary for its all-night singalongs and drinking. According to musician friends on this trip, Peggy was insulted by a drunken Australian who said: 'Give us a tune luv,' pointing to the piano. Peggy was indignant and retorted curtly: 'Luv doesn't do tunes.' The laughter along the carriage softened her. She had a habit of screwing up her nose whenever she was victorious and uttering a brief giggle, and she did this now. For all her aristocratic ways, underneath she was a good sport, although this quality was never predictable.

In 1986 a double opera bill of *The Transposed Heads* and *The Glittering Gate* was performed at the Adelaide Festival. Produced on a shoestring budget, this was not to be Peggy's finest hour or ultimate homecoming celebration. One wonders whether a European composer would have attracted the necessary funds to produce a quality production. In many ways a bad production can be more damaging than none at all and according to Peggy the latter would have been preferred in this case. Journalist Tristram Cary in the publication *Opera Australia* criticised the State Opera of South Australia, saying: 'It was a nice idea to pay tribute to Australia's senior woman composer, but it should have been done properly instead of presenting cut-price, reach-me-down, under-rehearsed versions . . . Some of the stage effects would have been substandard in a village hall.'[2]

Not all the reviews were negative. The *Adelaide Advertiser* described Peggy's music as having the mark of genius. It complimented the singers and the music, and seemed to grasp that *The Glittering Gate* was, as intended, merely a curtain-raiser, an existential farce to precede *The Transposed Heads*.[3] The *Australian* could muster few positive comments, choosing instead to explain the libretto.[4] Mostly it attacked the composer. The *Adelaide Review* blamed the director, saying that the direction appeared uncertain.[5] Peggy was quietly disgusted and avoided discussion of the production thereafter.

Late in 1988, an envelope arrived from Pittsburgh for Peggy containing a cheque for $2,000 for what they called 'the greatest contribution to harp music'. This piece of work was almost thirty years old. Other small prizes came giving cause for celebration to the ageing composer. The Australian commission that Peggy had hoped for, however, was not forthcoming. She was now considered beyond writing music. It was painful for her. She could only work on *Becket* for two hours in the morning due to her failing eyesight, but her enthusiasm never waned, nor did her humour and enjoyment of artistic discussion with people.

On occasion Peggy's work would appear in Europe, the United States and Australia. In 1980 the Lincoln Centre in New York held a retrospective production of her music, and at the Melbourne Town Hall in 1985 *Letters From Morocco* got an airing. Usually someone would send Peggy a clipping of the details which she would in turn show to friends who visited. Often the clipping would disappear with a visitor and Peggy would forget all about it.

Overall, Peggy felt some misgivings about her return home. She felt she was not taken seriously in Australia. There were always a few loyal people to bolster her reputation but she was not offered any commissions. She believed this was because she had not been produced enough in Australia to be known. Music circles knew of her but the broader public did not. Her success in America and Europe counted for little in Australia. Her music was only occasionally played on radio. To one journalist she would display her pain and invisibility, to another she would joke about the pleasures of anonymity. But she did not always hide her discontent and some newspapers conveyed her views:

> I've been back five years and no-one is interested. It's very humiliating. I've bought a house and I've come with great expectations but I think I'll have to go again. I wanted to be known in my own country for what I have in fact done but it's not going to happen. In New York I had my hard times but when I'm there I feel good and they allow me to do so because they think I'm pretty good too!

Given her proud disposition it seems likely that she was gravely disappointed but didn't want to appear bitter, a quality her personality would not allow. Besides, she loved the Australia she had refound. It was vibrant and she wanted to be a part of this 'new world' she described. She was equally proud of the numerous composers who had grown up in her absence and enthusiastic about new works. For all these conflicting reasons Peggy did not return to New York but remained in Sydney, encouraging and assisting whomever she could in music. She earned enough income from royalties, and with a part-pension managed to maintain a relatively comfortable lifestyle.

During this ambiguous phase of her career, film directors started to make documentaries about her, while journalists described the composer variously as 'forgotten', 'unheralded', 'an untapped resource', 'the equivalent of Percy Grainger', 'the composer without honour in her own country', 'the forgotten figure in Australian musical history' and so on. The name Peggy Glanville-Hicks appeared in crossword puzzles, and in Australian and American quiz programs. The University of Sydney conferred on honorary doctorate on her, and this biography began to take shape.

Meanwhile Peggy lived in her little terrace in Ormond Street, Paddington; in what she felt to be relative anonymity. This was Peggy as I first met her to work on her opera *Becket* and later this biography. Between paragraphs and interviews, I climbed the ladder in her garden a hundred times at her instruction to clip the ivy that had grown too high, or snip back the rose bush that was overshadowing the fern.

Peggy's house reflected her many interests just as her former homes had done. She remained a keen collector of paintings, and in no time had established a warm friendship with the local gallery owner and art entrepreneur, Barry Stern. She would frequent his gallery, always asking to be invited to exhibitions ahead of the crowds in order to snap up a potential bargain. On many of these occasions I accompanied her and on the journey she would discuss everything from the collapse of the British empire to creativity, arts funding, artists, and her newly-appreciated women friends—a luxury she claimed she had overlooked in her earlier hectic life.

On one occasion we attended an exhibition by the Australian painter Deborah Cooper whom Peggy was very enthusiastic about. She had recommended Cooper to Barry Stern and bought some paintings of the young artist. This was typical of her generosity when she met an artist who attracted her attention. Peggy was delighted that women had come into their own, as she put it. She enjoyed the achievements of her female friends and especially liked to count up the world's female leaders as if it were public proof of some long-hidden private victory.

Peggy and I drove to these exhibitions in my old roofless car. At seventy-six Peggy could still hoist herself in and out of the Moke with ease; instructing as she went. On one particular rainy Sydney night she climbed aboard saying 'turn the wipers on faster'. It began to rain even more heavily but Peggy simply put her umbrella up and ordered me to drive on. 'Hurry', she would say, 'we don't want to be late. Someone will have bought everything up.' Her delicious laugh was infectious.

Artists of all types would visit her at the prescribed visiting times of eleven or five, to be offered a glass of brandy and soda, a fresh prawn or two, some corn chips and the compulsory sprouts. She had a curious habit of shelling each individual prawn for her guests. She would take a razor blade from a special place on the coffee table and carefully slice the back of each shell to remove the black thread from inside. 'He might have eaten a drunken sailor,' she would joke, before handing the limp offering back to the guest. This peculiar habit raised an eyebrow or two as did her sudden burst of piano playing mid-conversation. She found it necessary sometimes to demonstrate her musical concept in discussion. At times this could develop into an unexpected performance.

Some of these artists came to discuss their ideas, others for help in gaining an exhibition, a grant, a reference, or to have her hear or view their latest work. Some stayed for a few days at a time.

From 1986 on, Peggy was working slowly on her opera *Becket* and almost every conversation we had contained news of the latest development in the score. She would often call me at unusual hours to give me an update on its development. One morning a call came at six o'clock in the morning, only this time Peggy's voice was high-pitched and weary. Poo the poodle had died during the night.

Fearful for her well-being I gathered up a shovel and blanket and drove to Paddington. It was a winter morning and the sun was barely up. The poodle was spread out on the loungeroom floor, draped in a sheet of red, white and blue. 'The American flag,' I joked. 'Fitting,' said Peggy, with an earnestness I was afraid to mistake for humour, although her roguish eyes suggested otherwise.

We attempted to gather the dog up in the sheet by raising both corners of the material. The body was now stiff and heavy as stone, and would not budge, and neither of us were prepared to touch the corpse. We sat down on the couch to confer. She with a glass of brandy in hand, offering me one, so as 'to calm our nerves'. 'Perhaps we need a man,' I said shamefully. 'Fiddlesticks' she retorted adamantly, then sighed that long sigh of hers I had come to know so well. We waited, for perhaps thirty minutes in silence; all the while I smoked and she drank, the bottle progressively emptying. We tried lifting the cloth at either end again.

It was no use. She cocked her head around the end of the cloth, now raised above her head and whispered. 'Do you have a boyfriend?' 'No,' I answered, unwilling to enter another debate on physical weakness. She began prying, a habit I had not known her to stoop to. 'What about that lovely director, Peter McLean, who is making a movie of me? Perhaps I could persuade him to film this tragic event.'

I looked at her. I knew it was a trick but wanted to be free of this situation as much as she did. She knew her storytelling often worked. On numerous occasions, Peggy had fooled the bottle shop into delivering brandy to her home by telling grandiose lies such as: 'I'm in the middle of the most horrendous piece of composition with people arriving by the minute, you simply must deliver immediately.'

I called Peter McLean. The phone rang for an eternity, all the while Peggy insisted that I just wait a little longer. It was no use, he was out. We sat down again. Another drink was poured. She took down her blue address book and considered a call to 'one who would not judge'. Composer Ross Edwards, the name floated up from the book like a blessing. She called him, and he was sympathetic and available. Peggy directed me to the graveyard—her flower bed by the weeping willow. I dug a hole larger than I ever thought possible, under strict instructions: 'He doesn't want his head facing north, now dig back a bit. Oh you are a poppet!' Ross carried the heavyweight poodle and laid him down without fuss. He left, unaware of the level of intoxication of the two failed heroines.

I had worried unnecessarily over the effect Poo's death would have on Peggy's general state of well-being. Life continued as usual at Ormond Street. She continued to talk of *Becket*, working mostly in her head rather than on paper, 'hydraglyphics' as she called it.

Postcards continued to arrive from around the world with news from old and new friends in the arts. Virgil Thomson would ring from New York and gossip about the new world of music. Esther Rofe, Peggy's oldest friend, came to pay her a visit from Melbourne. Occasionally a warming letter would arrive from Paul Bowles in Tangiers and she would again imagine the chance of a visit from him.

By 1987 my weekly visits and outings had more to do with our friendship and less with the biography. Her seventy-fifth birthday arrived, and composer Peter Sculthorpe invited us both to a party at his house. Peter's mother, Edna Sculthorpe, whom Peggy always loved to chat with, came too. There were shrieks of laughter from the two women. Peggy would tease Edna, 'Leave all the cooking and cleaning to the men, there are surely enough of them here.' There were indeed many friends, musicians and composers present, all talking at once. Peggy was thrilled to have attracted all this attention. She placed herself in the corner of the room facing the courtyard. There, dressed in her wonderful gold brocade jacket and shocking red scarf and stockings, she held court, addressing everyone whose name escaped her as 'little one'. She entertained those gathered about her with incredible tales of success and famous encounters. In her hand, the much loved brandy and soda and on her face a cleverness and humour.

In September 1989, *Concertino da Camera* was performed in Melbourne at the Assembly Hall of the Uniting Church as part of the Spoleto Festival's lunchtime chamber music concerts. Sadly, this initiative came from a film director whose sole purpose was to use the footage as part of his documentary. None the less, Peggy attended and was pleased.

Nearing seventy-seven Peggy decided to make a will, leaving her estate as a 'composers' house', a generous last bequest to the future of music. On 25 June 1990 after spending a glorious day with Peggy at her home in Paddington I received a call late at night from her family in Melbourne. She had had a heart attack and was in St Vincent's Hospital, Sydney. That evening she died.

NOTES

1. Deborah Hayes, 'Peggy Glanville-Hicks', *Bio-Bibliography in Music Series*, No. 27, Greenwood Press, United Stated, 1990.
2. *Opera Australia*, March 1986.
3. *Adelaide Advertiser*, March 1986.
4. The *Australian*, 24 March 1986.
5. *Adelaide Review*, No. 25, April 1986, p. 23.

WARDS OF THE STATE
An Autobiographical Novella
ROBERT ADAMSON

She sat on the mudguard and let her hair roll forward; black hair fell down her face, but she didn't care abut the screaming going on all around her. She just wanted to keep moving, to get back into the car and go. Anywhere, what did it matter, as long as the road hissed behind her.

Robert Adamson's autobiography is a poetic evocation of his childhood and boyhood in Sydney and on the Hawkesbury River. It encompasses the teenage dreams — girls, cars and impending manhood — which drew him into the closed net of boys' homes and a criminal life. Adamson finds in writing both release and resolution.

'Adamson is probably the best lyric poet in the country. He can write about the natural world more convincingly than anyone else. But at the same time Adamson is completely contemporary in his verse technique. He is a sort of feral Mallarmé.'
JOHN FORBES, *MELBOURNE HERALD*